A plant farm in Singapore

A FISHKEEPER'S GUIDE TO

A magnificently planted aquarium

No. 16069

The splendid spectacle of healthy aquarium plants

A FISHKEEPER'S GUIDE TO

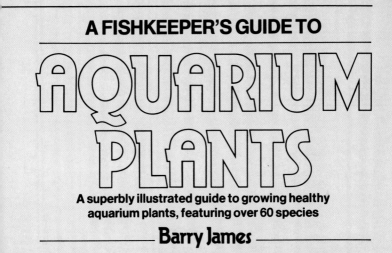

AQUARIUM PLANTS

A superbly illustrated guide to growing healthy aquarium plants, featuring over 60 species

— **Barry James** —

a Salamander book

Published by Salamander Books Limited
LONDON • NEW YORK

A Salamander Book

© 1986 Salamander Books Ltd.,
52 Bedford Row,
London WC1R 4LR,
United Kingdom.

ISBN 3-923880-57-X

This book may not be sold outside the United States of America.

All rights reserved. No part of this book
may be reproduced, stored in a retrieval system or transmitted
in any form or by any means, electronic, mechanical,
photocopying, recording or otherwise, without the
prior permission of Salamander Books Ltd.

All correspondence concerning the content of this volume
should be addressed to Salamander Books Ltd.

A superb display of plants above and below the water

Credits

Editor: Geoff Rogers   Designer: Tony Dominy
Colour reproductions:
Melbourne Graphics Ltd.
Filmset: SX Composing Ltd.
Printed in Belgium by Henri Proost & Cie, Turnhout.

Author

An early obsession with the natural world led Barry James to pursue botanical and zoological studies at London University. Using his wide experience of the commercial aquatic world, he opened his own aquatic nurseries some 14 years ago. Although still involved in the broader aspects of aquatics, his main interests have narrowed to the culture of aquatic plants, aquarium decor and oriental water gardening. He contributes regularly to the aquatic press, both as an author and photographer, and acts as a consultant worldwide to planning authorities, corporate bodies and private individuals on aquatic matters, including conservation projects.

Consultant

Fascinated by fishkeeping from early childhood, Dr. Neville Carrington devised an internationally known liquid food for young fishes while studying for a pharmacy degree. After obtaining his Doctorate in Pharmaceutical Engineering Science and a period in industry, Dr Carrington now pursues his life-long interest in developing equipment and chemical products for the aquarium world.

Contents

Introduction

Although enterprising gardeners in Europe have been cultivating aquatic plants in outdoor pools since the early eighteenth century, growing such plants in aquariums is a fairly recent phenomenon. The first real attempt to categorize aquatic plants came with the publication of Frances Perry's celebrated work 'Water Gardening' published in 1938. Since such pioneering works were published, much has been written on all aspects of aquatic plants. In recent years aquarists in continental Europe – especially in Holland and Germany – have led the way in exploring the secrets of how to grow these plants successfully. The parallel development of aquascaping – the use of gravel, rocks, bogwood and other materials to create attractive and life-like simulations of the natural environment in the confines of an aquarium – has completely transformed fishkeeping from being merely a 'pet-holding' exercise into one with limitless artistic horizons. In a well-planted and

aquascaped aquarium the fishes not only look better, with brighter and bolder colours, but they are also able to live a more natural and healthy existence than in stark, minimally decorated tanks. Indeed, in many cases the plants and aquascaping play a vital role in helping to establish breeding territories and spawning sites.

The key factor contributing to the explosion in the popularity of fishkeeping and growing aquarium plants has been the availability of a host of products and reliable technical aids to generate and maintain the correct environmental conditions necessary for both fishes and plants to prosper. These range from silicone sealant for bonding glass panels to complete life-support systems that monitor and control all the vital functions of an operating aquarium. In line with these trends, the first part of this book fully explores the application of modern technology to the art and science of growing aquarium plants.

The living plant

Before we discuss the techniques and equipment necessary to maintain healthy aquarium plants, let us look briefly at the fundamental processes that take place in living plants.

Plants range in structure from simple unicellular algae to complex higher plants composed of many different types of cells adapted to perform different functions. Thus, the roots, stems, branches, leaves, flowers and fruits all play their part in maintaining the whole plant. The two most vital processes that occur in all green plants, whether simple or complex in form, are photosynthesis and respiration.

Photosynthesis

As the term suggests, this is a building up process that is 'powered' by the energy of light. During photosynthesis, carbon dioxide is absorbed and oxygen liberated. These gases enter and leave the plant through tiny pores called stomata. Inside the plant cells – principally in the leaves – carbon dioxide and water are chemically combined in the presence of light and the green pigment chlorophyll to produce simple sugars, such as glucose. Although still imperfectly understood, the process can be simply expressed in the following equation:

$$6CO_2 + 6H_2O \xrightarrow[\text{Chlorophyll}]{\text{Light}}$$

Carbon dioxide   Water

$$C_6H_{12}O_6 + 6O_2$$

Glucose   Oxygen

The formation of simple sugars is quickly followed by other reactions that convert sugar into starch. Oxygen is produced as a by-product.

Photosynthesis is most active in the blue and red portions of the light

Below: *A healthy specimen of* Synnema triflorum. *Providing bright light not only powers the vital process of photosynthesis but, in this species, produces beautiful pinnate foliage.*

PHOTOSYNTHESIS RESPIRATION

NUTRIENTS NUTRIENTS

Above: *When the aquarium is lit, green aquatic plants absorb carbon dioxide and release oxygen as they photosynthesize. Inorganic nutrients enter by the roots and the leaves.*

Above: *When the aquarium is dark, photosynthesis stops but respiration continues, the plants using carbon dioxide and releasing oxygen. Less foods are respired than synthesized.*

spectrum, a factor to bear in mind when providing effective aquarium lighting (see page 20). It is the chlorophyll that absorbs these wavelengths to energize photosynthesis, although only about 3% of the light falling on a leaf is absorbed and used in this way.

Chlorophyll is really a mixture of two green pigments: chlorophyll a and chlorophyll b. Other plant pigments, such as carotene (orange) and xanthophyll (yellow), are masked by chlorophyll in green plants and are responsible for the striking patterns of variegated ones. They take no part in photosynthesis. A plant grown in the dark loses its chlorophyll, allowing other pigments to give it a sickly yellow 'etiolated' appearance.

For chlorophyll to form in the leaves a plant must have access to iron, hence the importance of providing sufficient iron in the substrate (see page 28, particularly the section on iron-rich clay soils). Plants lacking iron – said to be 'chlorotic' – assume a similar yellow or pale green appearance to etiolated plants, although the causes are quite different in the two instances.

The intensity of illumination, the supply of carbon dioxide and the temperature of the surroundings all affect the rate of photosynthesis. Between 0°C and 25°C (32-77°F), a rise of 10°C (18°F) effectively doubles the rate of photosynthesis. Similarly, a high concentration of carbon dioxide coupled with a high light intensity also produces a significant increase in photosynthetic activity. Thus, introducing carbon dioxide into the aquarium in carefully controlled amounts can boost plant growth in well-lit tanks.

Respiration

In simple terms, respiration is the reverse of photosynthesis. It is the process by which food substances are broken down in the presence of oxygen to liberate energy, principally as heat. Carbon dioxide is produced as a by-product. Respiration takes place in all plant cells and continues irrespective of light. Thus, during darkness – when photosynthesis ceases – respiration accounts for the net absorption of oxygen and the liberation of carbon dioxide from the plant, as shown in the diagram.

Water and fertilization

Aquatic organisms – whether they are plants or animals – are influenced to a greater or lesser extent by the physical, chemical and electrical properties of the water in which they live. Sphagnum mosses, for example, grow in highland areas with poor drainage, igneous rocks and low average temperatures. In these conditions, the water is soft and slightly acid. Taken from their natural habitat and placed in hard alkaline water, sphagnum mosses quickly die. Fortunately, most aquatic plants – including those used as aquarium subjects – are very adaptable to a wide variety of water conditions.

To grow more sensitive plants successfully in an aquarium, the water quality must closely simulate that of their natural environment. In addition to the water temperature (see Heating and lighting, page 20) and its 'cleanliness' (see Filtration, page 18), the most important aspects of water quality as far as plants (and fishes) are concerned are its hardness and its degree of acidity or alkalinity. Here we briefly consider these parameters and how they are measured.

Water hardness

To understand how water becomes hard or soft, we must break into the natural water cycle as rainwater falls through the atmosphere. On its downward journey, rain reacts with small amounts of carbon dioxide to produce carbonic acid, as shown below:

$$CO_2 + H_2O \rightarrow H_2CO_3$$
Carbon   Water   Carbonic
dioxide   acid

This simple reaction is the key to many changes that occur when rainwater becomes groundwater. As we have seen in our example of sphagnum mosses, where rainwater falls on hard, igneous (and therefore, inert) rocks the groundwater remains low in dissolved mineral salts – i.e. 'soft' and slightly acidic. (In fact, organic acids from dead and decaying plants also add to the acidity of the water.) But where the slightly acidic rainwater flows through sedimentary rocks, such as chalk and limestone, further chemical reactions occur that add 'hardness' to the water. The basic reaction involves the action of carbonic acid on calcium carbonate (chalk) to produce calcium bicarbonate, as shown below:

$$H_2CO_3 + CaCO_3 \rightarrow Ca(HCO_3)_2$$
Carbonic   Calcium   Calcium
acid   carbonate bicarbonate

Equivalent reactions involve magnesium carbonate.

Since the bicarbonates produced can be easily broken down by boiling, this type of hardness is called temporary hardness or carbonate hardness. (It is normally designated as KH.) As the bicarbonates decompose, the carbonate portion is deposited as white scale – a familiar sight inside kettles for people living in hard water areas. (The level of bicarbonates in water is also important for aquarists because they act as a 'storage area' for carbon dioxide and help to stabilize the acidity/alkalinity balance of the water.)

But calcium and magnesium carbonates are not the only mineral salts involved in producing water hardness. Reactions with other naturally occurring compounds in rocks produce a veritable 'cocktail' of mineral salts, so that hard water may contain the sulphates, carbonates,

Below: *The abundant plant growth bordering this Brazilian stream thrives in the rich soil beneath its dark, soft and acidic waters.*

Water hardness in comparative terms

°dH	Mg/litre CaCO₃	Considered as
3	0-50	Soft
3-6	50-100	Moderately soft
6-12	100-200	Slightly hard
12-18	200-300	Moderately hard
18-25	300-450	Hard
Over 25	Over 450	Very hard

Several scales are used to express water hardness. Here, we compare the widely used German scale of °dH with an alternative scale based on milligrams of calcium carbonate (CaCO₃) per litre of water.

bicarbonates, nitrates and chlorides of calcium, magnesium, barium and strontium. The level of hardness produced by the sum total of these substances is called, quite logically, the total or general hardness (GH).

Water hardness is measured in a confusing range of units. In this book we have used the German scale of °dH, which can be applied either to general hardness or to carbonate hardness. As far as aquarium plants are concerned, carbonate hardness is the most significant of the two parameters. Alternatively, general hardness can be expressed in terms of milligrams per litre of calcium carbonate (mg/l CaCO₃).

For convenience, the table shows the comparative levels of hardness in both these scales.

The fraction of general hardness that cannot be removed by boiling is called permanent hardness and is caused mainly by calcium sulphate.

Most of our tropical aquarium plants come from areas of soft water, whereas some from subtropical areas grow in relatively hard water. In practice, most plants adapt very well to growing in domestic tapwater, which is invariably hardened to reduce corrosion in metal pipes. Where this is the case, we have used the term 'not critical' against the recommended hardness level for each plant in Part Two of the book. Where necessary, we have quoted the desired hardness range in °dH.

Various test kits are widely available for measuring the hardness of water. Most involve counting the number of drops of a reagent needed to change the colour of an indicator added to a measured water sample. Electronic meters that register hardness by measuring the electrical conductivity of the water give accurate and speedy results, but are relatively expensive and delicate pieces of equipment for the aquarist.

pH scale

0 1 2 3 4 5 6 7 8 9 10 11 12 13 14

Neutral

Extremely acidic

Extremely alkaline

Acidity and alkalinity

Describing water as either 'acidic' or 'alkaline' is relative in terms of a 'neutral' point. The universally accepted way of expressing this aspect of water quality is in terms of pH value. The pH scale is a logarithmic calibration based inversely on the concentration of hydrogen ions in the water. Thus, the more hydrogen ions there are in the water the greater is its acidity and the lower its rating on the pH scale. On the scale, pH 7 is neutral, with values

from 7 down to 0 denoting increasing acidity and those from 7 to 14 signifying increasing alkalinity. The logarithmic nature of the scale means that one whole number step represents a ten-fold variation, two steps represent a hundred-fold variation and three steps a thousand-fold variation, etc.

Aquarium plants are not as drastically affected by violent changes in pH values as are most fishes, although some authorities suggest that so-called 'cryptocoryne rot' is caused by rapid variations in pH level. Most aquarium plants will thrive in water with a pH value in the range 6.5-7.4. In Part Two of the book we have quoted more precise pH levels where desirable for certain species. Otherwise, the term 'not critical' implies that a species will adapt to a reasonable range of pH values.

As for water hardness, easy-to-use test kits are available for measuring pH value. These include kits using liquid reagents as well as paper strips impregnated with suitable indicators.

Above: *Taking regular readings of pH value is very easy with modern test kits. Here, paper strips treated with an indicator provide instant results. Other kits use liquid reagents added to a small sample of tank water.*

Fertilization

Chemical analysis reveals that plant material contains not only oxygen, hydrogen and carbon, but also nitrogen, chlorine, sulphur, phosphorus, potassium, sodium, calcium, magnesium, iron, manganese, silicon, iodine, copper, zinc and boron in varying amounts. These elements are obtained from the substrate by means of the roots but are also absorbed by aquatic plants directly through their leaves and shoots from the water.

As in land plants, the major nutrients for aquatic plants are nitrates, sulphates and phosphates. Taken in as simple inorganic substances, the plant transforms them into more complex compounds by the catalytic process of photosynthesis and ultimately by enzyme action into the amino-acids and proteins that form plant protoplasm.

Basic research has shown that streams in which plants grow are continuously fertilized by underground sources of water containing concentrated quantities of nutrients. These include not only the major nutrients but also the so-called trace elements, such as iron, manganese, zinc, copper and boron. Many of these elements are vital to plant growth because they are incorporated into the molecular structure of enzymes that facilitate the chemical reactions of plant metabolism. Plants lacking these vital elements suffer from 'deficiency' diseases. Even so, only the minutest amounts of these elements are needed (hence 'trace' elements); larger concentrations can be lethal.

The clay soils common in tropical regions – often seen as a red sludge overlying stream and river beds – are particularly rich in iron. This is present in an active form – so-called 'nutrient iron' – that enables other vital elements to be absorbed in a soluble form by the plants. (The role of clay soils in aquarium substrates is further discussed on page 28.)

When domestic tapwater is used in the aquarium, abundant supplies of nitrates, phosphates and sulphates are usually present. These are derived, in part, from seepage from farming land that has been treated with fertilizers. Sometimes, the amounts are so excessive as to be toxic to the aquarium plants or to cause 'algal blooms' (see page 47). Nitrates also build up naturally in an aquarium stocked with fishes as bacteria break down their waste products (see page 19).

For an aquarium filled with mains water, therefore, an all-round plant fertilizer is not really necessary since many of the nutrients are present in sufficient or over-abundant concentrations already. A fertilizer is required simply to 'fill the gaps' left in the composition of the mains water. As regular water changes are necessary to counteract the gradual build-up of inorganic wastes in the aquarium, it is usually the levels of trace elements that must be made good at these times. Where rainwater is used, an all-round 'physiologically balanced' fertilizer is necessary. Fertilizers suitable for both instances are widely available in liquid and tablet form from aquarium dealers.

Below: *To help new plants establish and grow away strongly, add root activating tablets to the gravel and liquid fertilizer to the water.*

Using carbon dioxide

For many years it has been standard practice in horticulture to use carbon dioxide generators in greenhouses to boost the growth rate of both ornamental and food plants. It follows, therefore, that introducing extra carbon dioxide into well-lit and well-nourished aquariums will benefit aquarium plants in the same way by maximising the overall rate of photosynthesis.

There are several systems available for introducing carbon dioxide into aquarium water, varying in sophistication. The important point to consider is the concentration of the gas. The optimum level is 5-15mg per litre of tank water, with a maximum of 20mg/l. Avoid introducing excessive levels of carbon dioxide because of the possible detrimental effect on the fishes.

The level of carbon dioxide also affects the pH value and carbonate hardness of the water. As plants use the carbon dioxide in the water for photosynthesis – initially as CO_2 gas and then by extracting CO_2 from calcium bicarbonate – the pH value rises. Adding extra CO_2 causes the pH value to fall.

In their natural habitat, aquatic plants become adapted to the fluctuations in pH value that occur because of the variations in such factors as CO_2 level, carbonate hardness, water temperature, light intensity, water movement, concentration of plant life, etc. In the closed confines of an aquarium, it is easy to disrupt the natural balance between these factors by introducing too much CO_2 in a single-minded attempt to increase photosynthetic activity. But, handled carefully, there is no doubt that such techniques are beneficial in providing vital supplies of the element carbon to the plants.

The systems available for adding CO_2 vary from simple 'manual' ones to those linked to the lighting system (CO_2 is turned off when the lights turn off) and those with complex feed back arrangements involving automatic pH monitoring. Whatever system is used, it is always a good idea to test the water for CO_2 level, and test kits are available for this, such as Tetra Test.

Filtration

The primary function of filtration is to remove unwanted substances from the aquarium in order to improve the clarity of the water for the well-being of the fishes and plants the aquarium contains. Many types of filters can also be used to alter the quality of aquarium water by *adding* substances to promote fish health and reproductive activity as well as to activate and improve plant growth.

Aquarium filters achieve these effects in three basic ways: by mechanical, chemical and biological action. The distinction between these activities often breaks down in reality because many filtration systems carry out all three functions at the same time. Let us look briefly at the filtration systems available to fishkeepers and consider how appropriate they are for promoting healthy plant growth in the aquarium.

Mechanical filtration

Filters rarely operate on a purely mechanical basis because, once established, they usually exert a chemical and/or biological influence on the water passing through them. Simple foam filters, air-operated box filters and power filters are all basically mechanical filters.

Mechanical filters have the advantage of efficiently removing floating debris which would block up the pores of aquarium plants, especially the fine-leaved species such as *Myriophyllum, Limnophila*, etc. The faster turnover of power filters – basically canisters filled with filter medium and driven by electric pumps – also disturbs the heavier detritus that accumulates on the substrate. Removing this layer not only improves the appearance of the aquarium but also increases the overall lighting level in an aquarium by exposing the reflective gravel layer (see also page 26). Extending the return flow pipe of a power filtration system with suitable extra tubes and bends can set up underwater currents in the aquarium that help to remove debris more effectively and cause the plants to sway in a very realistic way. And many fishes seem to enjoy swimming against such powerful streams.

Chemical filtration

Chemical filters are often incorporated within or attached to mechanical filters. Activated carbon and zeolite, for example, are two widely available substances that make up part of the filter media in a wide range of filters and serve to remove dissolved waste products and other chemicals from the water.

Putting fibrous peat into a filter releases tannic and humic acids into the water. These lower the pH value of soft waters and have a softening effect on hard waters. Vitamins and hormones are also released from the peat and these have a beneficial effect on both fishes and plants in the aquarium.

Water softening resins can also be considered as chemical filters. The type used in domestic water softeners are not suitable for aquarium use, however, because they substitute the calcium ions of water hardness with sodium ions and these make the water excessively alkaline. The so-called 'de-ionising resins' are almost too efficient because they produce chemically pure water that must be diluted with other water supplies (thereby softening them) before being used in the aquarium.

Biological filtration

Biological filters harness the natural ability of bacteria to break down harmful substances that build up in the aquarium water. The most important substances involved form part of the nitrogen cycle. Thus, waste products produced by the fishes and decaying plant and animal remains are decomposed by natural bacterial action into ammonia (NH_3) and ammonium compounds. Since ammonia and similar compounds are highly toxic to all living organisms, it is essential for a biological filter to encourage the growth of various types of bacteria – so-called nitrifying bacteria – that decompose these compounds to less harmful substances. The bacteria concerned include *Nitrosomonas* sp., which oxidises ammonia and similar compounds to less toxic nitrites (NO_2) and *Nitrobacter* sp., which takes the

active' surface. Media commonly used include aquarium gravel, crushed volcanic rock, ceramic or plastic pieces, activated carbon and foam. Foam, in particular, has a very high internal surface area and is ideal for supporting bacterial growth. Foam filters can be used in various ways, from small self-contained devices powered by simple air uplift to large foam cartridges fitted into power filters. Whatever medium is used, however, the aim is to provide an oxygen-rich environment in which the useful aerobic bacteria can flourish.

The design and operation of various biological filters differ quite considerably, but all work on the same basic principle.

The most widely used biological filtration system is the undergravel filter. In this system, the aquarium gravel bed is used as the bacterially active medium. In the usual arrangement, water is drawn down through the gravel to a filter plate at the base of the aquarium and then circulated back into the tank near the water surface. This water flow can be set up either by using a simple airlift or a power head pump. As the water passes through the gravel, the bacteria break the toxic substances down into nitrates.

Undergravel filters are not conducive to good plant growth, however, and are not compatible with nutrient-rich materials, such as iron-rich clay soil, placed under the gravel; the downward flow of water through the filter simply draws down such material and spreads it all over the tank, creating a mess. Also, for reasons not yet completely understood, undergravel filters appear to inhibit aquarium plants from absorbing certain vital nutrients. As a result, the plants may become stunted and pale yellow in colour, indicating that photosynthesis is somehow disrupted.

The less widely seen, but more efficient, drip-feed types of biological filters enable the oxygen threshold to be greatly increased and do not have the same harmful side-effects that may be experienced with standard undergravel filters.

Above: *Foam filters strain dirt particles mechanically and also support biologically active bacteria that break down toxic aquarium wastes. To clean them, simply detach and wash the foam cartridge.*

decomposition process still further by oxidising nitrites to the much less toxic nitrates (NO_3). Nitrates are, in turn, absorbed by plants as a source of nitrogen. Fishes, however, suffer in increasing levels of nitrates and regular partial water changes are necessary to keep these levels within acceptable limits for the aquarium occupants.

All biological filters contain an inert medium that will provide a large surface area to support bacterial growth, in essence a 'bacterially

Heating and lighting

Research in many tropical countries has shown that the average temperature of the water hovers around 24-26°C (75-79°F). (In the aquarium most tropical and subtropical plants will flourish at 24-28°C/75-82°F). There seems to be scarcely any temperature difference between the moving waters of rivers and streams and the still waters of ponds and lakes. Nor is there any appreciable drop in temperature during the night. Thus, there is no need to adopt lower night temperatures in the tropical aquarium.

There are three alternative methods of recreating the warmth of the tropics in the confines of an aquarium:

1 Using a conventional heater-thermostat
2 Supplying heat from beneath the aquarium
3 Installing a thermofilter

Let us consider the merits and possible problems of these three systems.

Heater-thermostats
The conventional heater-thermostats are perfectly adequate for plant growth. As a guide, allow 10 watts for every 4.5 litres (1 gallon) of water in the aquarium. Thus, a 60cm (24in) aquarium holding 54-68 litres (12-15 gallons) of water will need a heater-thermostat rated at 120-150 watts. Since these devices are available in standard output ratings, choose the nearest one to your calculated needs. Preferably, choose a slightly more powerful one if your calculation leads to an 'in-between' figure. For large tanks – in excess of 90cm (36in) long – use two heater-thermostats wired in parallel to make up the total required wattage. Place these at opposite ends of the aquarium to ensure an even distribution of heat.

Heating from below
Supplying heat from beneath the aquarium, either in the form of an electrically heated pad under the tank base or as an electrical heating element buried in the gravel, can keep

the plant roots warm and induce excellent plant growth. To keep a check on the temperature of the substrate, fix a liquid crystal thermometer horizontally on the outside of the tank near the base.

Thermofilter
In a thermofilter system the heating and thermostatic elements are housed in an external power filter. This ensures excellent distribution of heat around the aquarium, but problems could arise if the pump fails.

Lighting
Plant life has been evolving under the sun for millions of years. It follows, therefore, that natural sunlight is the perfect form of illumination for aquarium plants. Natural daylight, however, is difficult to control as its intensity varies from day to day depending on the season, cloud cover, time of day and degree of atmospheric pollution, etc. And without any control over the amount of light the aquarium receives, blooms of unwelcome algae may develop in excessively bright conditions. It is necessary, therefore, to use artificial forms of light in aquariums. Fortunately, over the past 20 years or so, many new forms of lighting have become available that lend themselves to aquarium use. By carefully controlling the quality, intensity and duration of the light, it is possible to achieve perfect aquarium plant growth using purely artificial light sources.

Quality of light
Visible light forms only a narrow segment of total electromagnetic radiation, which ranges from extremely short cosmic rays to long radio waves and beyond. The familiar visible spectrum of violet to red light occupies a portion of wavelengths from 380 to 780 nanometers. (A nanometer, usually abbreviated to nm, is a billionth part of a metre.) Just as the human eye varies in its sensitivity to different wavelengths, so chlorophyll in plants also absorbs the spectral components of light to varying degrees. The absorption spectrum for chlorophyll shows

noticeable peaks in the violet-blue (380-480nm) and orange-red (600-680nm) regions, which also mark – as you would expect – peaks in photosynthetic activity. (That plants reflect most of the green light and absorb relatively little is clear from their apparent green colour to our eyes.) For plants to prosper under artificial light it follows, therefore, that the most effective light sources will be those that produce a large portion of their light in the blue and orange-red regions of the visible spectrum.

Intensity of light

It is very difficult to judge the brightness of a light source; it all depends on the background level of illumination. In pitch darkness a car headlamp, for example, may seem dazzling, whereas in full daylight it appears very dim. To understand the way brightness is calibrated we must introduce two units of measurement. The amount of light produced by a light source is measured in units known as lumens. (The number of lumens produced per watt of power applied to a lamp is a measure of its

Above: *Whatever form of aquarium heating is used, it is a good idea to monitor the temperature of the substrate and the water separately.*

Below: *The spectral energy curve of sunlight (white) peaks at 475nm; the plant sensitivity for photosynthesis (black) peaks at 675nm.*

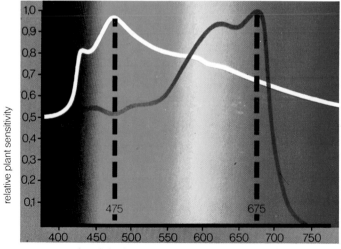

These same scales are used on the graphs shown on page 27

efficiency. In general terms, an incandescent lamp is less efficient than a fluorescent tube because a greater portion of the power applied to the former is converted into heat rather than light.) The amount of light reaching a surface is measured in lux, which is equivalent to lumens per square metre. Lux is measured with a

Above: *A healthy specimen of* Ceratophyllum submersum *grown at an ideal lighting level in the aquarium.*

luxmeter or lightmeter. (A standard photographic exposure meter can be used to measure lux by converting the diaphragm and exposure times.)

Plants vary widely in their light intensity requirements. Aquatic plants growing in the deep shade of a forest pool flourish at far lower light levels than those adapted to live in the shallows of streams open to the sky. And land plants that live in the full

---

Light requirements of selected aquarium plants

Under 500 lux / Subdued
Cryptocoryne affinis
Cryptocoryne nevillii
Cryptocoryne wendtii
Vesicularia dubyana

500-1000 lux / Moderate
Acorus sp.
Anubias nana
Aponogeton madagascariensis
Echinodorus sp.
Lagenandra sp.
Nomaphila stricta
Sagittaria sp.

1000-1500 lux / Bright
Aponogeton sp.
Bacopa caroliniana
Ceratopteris thalictroides
Egeria densa
Ludwigia sp.
Marsilea sp.
Nymphoides aquatica

1500+ lux / Very bright
Cabomba sp.
Heteranthera zosterifolia
Hygrophila polysperma
Limnobium laevigatum
Limnophila aquatica
Microsorium pteropus
Myriophyllum sp.
Nuphar sagittifolium
Nymphaea maculata
Pistia stratiotes
Riccia fluitans
Salvinia auriculata
Synnema triflorum
Vallisneria sp.

Land plants
Succulents 9,000-14,000 lux
Young trees 10,000-15,000 lux
Cereals 50,000-60,000 lux

AQUARIUM PLANTS –

Aquarium capacity		
Litres	Imp. gals	US gals
71	15.6	18.7
85	18.7	22.4
88	19.4	23.3
106	23.3	28.0
110	24.2	29.0
142	31.2	37.4
160	35.2	42.2
200	44.0	52.8
263	57.9	69.5
321	70.6	84.7
400	88.0	105.6
480	105.6	126.7

Above: *In too little light, the same plant is pale green and shows elongated growth between nodes.*

Above: *Too much light causes the foliage to take on an unattractive 'bleached out' appearance.*

glare of the sun absorb surprisingly high lux levels. The table on page 22 lists the lux requirements of a representative selection of aquarium plants, plus some land plants for comparison. Fortunately, most aquarium plants have similar requirements and/or are adaptable within a specific range. Thus, it is usually possible to grow different species with varying lighting needs

together in the same aquarium. The individual species descriptions in Part Two include an indication of the ideal light intensity for each plant. These are categorised in the same comparative terms used in the table opposite.

Below: *This table provides a general guide to lighting a planted aquarium with fluorescent tubes. Ideally, use tubes with a balanced light output.*

Recommended lighting levels

Length × Depth × Width in cms	Length × Depth × Width in in.	No. of tubes	Length of tubes
60×38×30	24×15×12	3×15 watt	45cm/18in
70×35×35	28×14×14	2×20 watt	60cm/24in
75×38×30	30×15×12	3×20 watt	60cm/24in
90×38×30	36×15×12	2×25 watt	75cm/30in
70×35×45	28×14×18	3×20 watt	60cm/24in
120×38×30	48×15×12	2×40 watt	107cm/42in
100×40×40	39×16×16	2×30 watt	90cm/36in
100×40×50	39×16×20	3×30 watt	90cm/36in
130×45×45	51×18×18	2×40 watt	120cm/48in
130×45×55	51×18×22	3×40 watt	120cm/48in
160×50×50	63×20×20	2×65 watt	150cm/60in
160×50×60	63×20×24	2×65 watt	150cm/60in

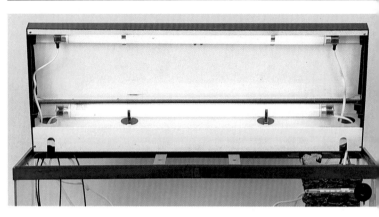

Above: *Most aquarium hoods can be fitted with two fluorescent tubes – an ideal arrangement. Here, tubes of different colour give balanced light.*

Below: *Lighting an open-top aquarium with high intensity metal-halide lamps can produce healthy plant growth and a stunning display.*

The duration of light

Tropical plants are known as 'short day plants'. This is because in the areas of the world close to the equator, day and night are divided approximately into two periods of twelve hours each. Of the twelve hours that the sun shines in a tropical day, sunset and sunrise occupy a period of one hour each. This leaves ten hours of intense light. This period, the so-called 'photoperiod', is the length of time you should leave the lights on in the aquarium for tropical plants to 'feel at home'.

Also remember, however, that the period of darkness is even more critical than the photoperiod. During darkness, respiration is at its highest level. Oxygen is absorbed and carbon dioxide released. The sugar stored in

the cells is oxidized according to the following equation:

$$C_6H_{12}O_6 + 6O_2 \rightarrow 6CO_2 + 6H_2O + 674 \text{ calories}$$

Having looked briefly at the quality, brightness and duration of lighting required for healthy plant growth, let us consider how well the various types of lamps currently available perform in this respect.

Tungsten bulbs and tubes

It is possible to grow plants under tungsten (incandescent) lamps but they do lack the blue end of the spectrum and give out a great deal of their energy as heat, with its attendant problems. They are inefficient and thus relatively expensive to run and have a comparatively short life. Incandescent lamps have been largely superseded by a wide range of fluorescent tubes.

Fluorescent tubes

A fluorescent tube contains mercury vapour, which glows when it becomes electrically charged and emits light mainly in the ultraviolet range. This invisible light energy is transformed into visible light as it strikes a coating of fluorescent material on the inside surface of the tube. Depending on the chemical formulation of the coating used, the spectrum of visible light produced can be fine tuned to suit particular applications.

The lighting industry has developed many types of fluorescent tubes to suit a variety of purposes, such as shop signs, domestic and industrial lighting, etc. A great deal of research has also gone into producing tubes for the horticultural industry for the intensive propagation of ornamental and food crops under glass and in growing rooms used for horticultural research purposes.

The benefits of this research and experimentation are now available to aquarists in the wide choice of fluorescent tubes that can be used to promote healthy and active plant growth in the aquarium. Some of these tubes are specifically marketed for aquarium use.

Certain other tubes not specifically designed for growing plants produce a balanced light output that closely simulates natural daylight and thus can be strongly recommended.

As well as producing light in useful spectral ranges for plant growth, fluorescent tubes are preferable to incandescent lamps because they run cool, consume relatively little electricity and are long-lasting. Some tubes incorporate a 'power twist', which is literally a twist in the glass that exposes a greater surface area of tube to boost light output for the same electrical power input.

Metal-halide lamps
Metal-halide lamps (variously called tungsten-halogen or quartz-halogen lamps) are relatively expensive, but they do give a high light output at modest running costs. The tungsten filament in these lamps glows extremely brightly, producing a strong white light. Any tungsten that evaporates combines with the iodine or bromine (the halogen) inside the quartz envelope and is re-deposited on to the filament.

They are available in special reflector fittings with a variety of decorative finishes. Use them in open-top tanks with no canopy, and suspend the fittings from the ceiling on chains or spiral leads. Fitted 30cm (12in) above the surface of the water, one 150 watt lamp will illuminate a surface area of 1800 cm^2 (approximately 2ft^2). Metal-halide lamps will punch light to a depth of 70cm (26in), for example, and so are ideal for deep tanks.

Mercury vapour lamps
Mercury vapour lamps (as opposed to fluorescent tubes) also produce high intensity output and are a little cheaper to buy than metal-halide lamps. Again, they are usually suspended over open-top aquariums and are available in several power ratings to suit most situations.

So-called 'blended-light' lamps containing both an incandescent filament and a high-pressure mercury discharge tube produce an excellent spectral output for plant growth and are available with a built-in reflector.

Avoid looking directly at any of these high-intensity light sources.

High-pressure sodium lamps
In these lamps a coating of sodium on the inside of the tube glows brightly once heated for several minutes by an initial discharge. As it warms up, the lamp glows at first red and then orange-red. Although widely used commercially and in horticulture, high-pressure sodium lamps are less commonly used for home aquariums. The orange-red bias of the light output can be balanced by using a metal-halide lamp to boost the blue content of the spectrum.

Light losses
The loss of light intensity is a very important factor that many aquarists overlook. When the aquarium is first set up the water is crystal clear, the condensation trays are new and polished, and the tubes are fresh from the supplier. In these early days, the maximum amount of light possible reaches the plants. However, gradually the tubes become coated in dust and fall off in brightness, and the condensation trays become obscured by the deposition of lime scale from evaporated water droplets. If the filters are not working efficiently, the water may accumulate a mass of finely suspended matter that disperses light passing through it. Mulm – a layer of organic debris – forms on the base, masking the reflective capacity of the gravel and, worst of all, the water may become discoloured due to the accumulation of organic wastes, from the introduction of insufficiently washed bogwood or by the excessive use of the so-called 'blackwater' tonics which contain various plant and peat extracts to treat the water.

All these obstructions reduce the luminous intensity reaching the plants by an enormous amount. Even clean water and glass absorb light to some extent, so it is not difficult to imagine the effects of these cumulative influences. To maintain lighting levels in the aquarium be sure to make regular water changes, service filters, and keep all the tank accessories and equipment as clean as possible.

Fluorescent

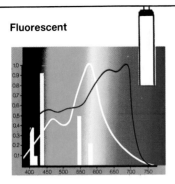

Above: *Fluorescent tubes are ideal for plant growth. This output shows mercury discharge as bars, light from the fluorescent layer as a curve.*

Incandescent

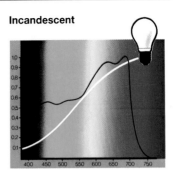

Above: *Although inexpensive and easy to install, incandescent lamps produce a spectral output weighted towards the red part of the spectrum.*

High-pressure mercury

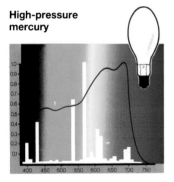

Above: *These lamps produce a useful light output and have been widely used in horticulture. Other lamps are now gradually taking their place.*

Blended-light

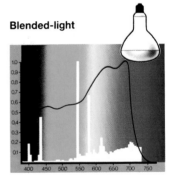

Above: *The combination of tungsten and mercury elements in these lamps ensures a balanced light output for plant growth. Easy to use.*

Metal-halide

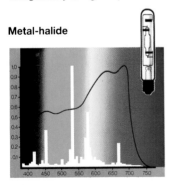

Above: *High-pressure metal-halide lamps produce very bright light for their size and power input. Ideal for plants needing high light intensity.*

High-pressure sodium

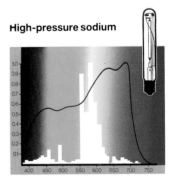

Above: *Although low in blue light, these compact lamps are efficient and long-lasting. Balance the light by combining with metal-halide lamps.*

The substrate

Since the substrate forms the anchor and growing medium for plant roots, it is vital to choose a material, or combination of materials, that will not only sustain the plants both mechanically and nutritionally, but also look attractive as part of the tank decor. Here, we consider the options available for successful plant growth.

Gravel

Gravel is the universal substrate in aquarium circles. It can be used as the sole substrate in planted aquariums, although it is best employed as a top layer covering areas or 'pockets' of nutritious growing medium beneath.

The most popular type of gravel is low-calcium beach gravel with a particle size of 2-3mm (0.08-0.1in). This grade allows roots to penetrate easily and yet provides a firm support for the plants.

Baked clay gravels are also available. These are larger in particle size, brown to deep brown in colour and, since they do not contain calcium, they do not affect the hardness or pH value of the water. These gravels are pre-packed and are often impregnated with trace elements by the suppliers, thus making them an ideal plant growing medium. Their highly porous structure also provides an excellent 'home' for nitrifying bacteria in biological filter systems.

Peat

Loose sphagnum moss peat was once widely used as a growing medium beneath gravel. Using loose peat has its disadvantages, however, mainly because of its tendency to disintegrate and disperse around the aquarium. New growing media are available that do not suffer from these problems and are optimised to encourage good plant growth.

Gravel additives

The iron-rich clay soils found in some tropical areas, often imparting a reddish colour to the bed of streams and pools, can be especially valuable in promoting lush plant growth. The iron compounds dissolve from such soils and combine with organic acids produced by the plant roots. This 'organic iron' is not only more easily absorbed by plants but it also enables other trace elements the soil contains (and which are normally 'locked up' in stable compounds) to be released and made available for plant growth.

Several commercially produced substrate additives incorporate such iron-rich clay in their formulation. Using these additives is simply a question of adding the material to about 75% of the washed gravel and using the remaining gravel as a top cover. Add the supplied fertilizer tablets as directed – broken up and inserted in the gravel near the roots – to encourage healthy root growth. A suitable liquid fertilizer can be added to promote the development of leaves and stems.

Rock wool hydroculture

Rock wool – a fluffy greyish substance – is an ideal growing medium for plants set in hydroculture

Below: *Aquarium plants grown in slatted hydroculture pots. These help plants to become established and allow easy removal and repositioning.*

Gravel additive for naturally planted aquariums.
Establishes aquarium gravel for initial growth
and full development of aquatic plants.

pots. These are plastic pots with an open lattice structure that allows the plant roots to extend outwards into the main tank substrate. The rock wool, impregnated with a suitable fertilizer, acts as an inert support for the roots as they absorb essential nutrients. For aquarium use, wrap the roots in rock wool and insert each plant into a pot before setting it into the substrate. Small pots of 4cm (1.6in) diameter are ideal.

Above: *Use gravel additives (prepared from nutrient-rich soils) by mixing them with the aquarium gravel as directed. Insert pieces of root activating tablets close to the plants.*

Below: *Various grades of aquarium gravel plus two colours of baked clay, fertilizer-impregnated substrates. The two finer grades of gravel are usually the most suitable to support good growth in aquarium plants.*

Aquascaping

When you are furnishing and planting an aquarium – a pursuit appropriately known as 'aquascaping' – your first considerations must centre around the position of the tank in the room and its size and accessibility.

Viewpoint and site

Most aquariums are viewed from the front and sides only, with the back against a wall. As a variation on this theme, the tank can be let into a wall or partition, with only the front panel exposed. Alternatively, used as a room divider, an aquarium may have the two long sides and one end on show. And to take things to their logical conclusion, an aquarium may well occupy a central position and be viewed from all round. Remember

Below: *This beautifully furnished freshwater tropical aquarium provides an excellent focal point in the room, a fitting reward for hard work.*

that all these possibilities demand a different approach when it comes to aquascaping and you should tailor the general advice given here to fit your chosen site and position.

When selecting an aquarium, do bear in mind that it will prove difficult to plant up tanks over 60cm (24in) deep by hand.

Essential planning

Before doing anything else, draw up a plan of how you see the finished aquarium in your mind's eye. It is rather like planning a garden, only on a smaller scale. You do not need to be an artist to prepare a simple sketch – ideally in plan and front views. Look up the size and shape of the plants you consider suitable (see pages 59-113) and draw in the areas they will occupy in relation to the 'hard' furnishings in the aquarium.

To help you make a sensible choice, aquarium plants can be

classified according to their form, size and growing characteristics into the following categories:

Floating plants: These, as their name suggests, float on or just below the water surface. Many contain spongy air-filled cells that provide the necessary buoyancy. Some have long roots that hang down in the water that serve as spawning sites for fishes and as refuges for the resulting fry. All floating plants afford shade to the other plants and fishes in the aquarium. The floating plants featured in this book are: *Limnobium laevigatum, Pistia stratiotes, Riccia fluitans* and *Salvinia auriculata*.

Bunch plants: So-called because they are best planted in 'bunches' of rootless top cuttings (see page 52), these plants root in the substrate and grow towards the surface without any definite limit to their spread. They

consist of long stems with the leaves arranged in opposition, alternately or in whorls, and they are ideal for planting as a background in the aquarium. Typical bunch plants featured include: *Ammannia senegalensis, Bacopa caroliniana, Cabomba caroliniana, Cardamine lyrata, Egeria densa, Gymnocoronis spilanthoides, Heteranthera zosterifolia, Hottonia inflata, Hygrophila polysperma, Limnophila aquatica, Ludwigia mullertii, Myriophyllum hippuroides, Nomaphila stricta, Rotala macrandra, Synnema triflorum* and *Trichoronis rivularis*.

Specimen plants: Normally large and imposing, these species are usually planted in the middleground of the aquarium to create a striking design feature. Most plants used as specimens produce leaves in a rosette formation. Typical examples featured in Part Two of the book

include: *Aponogeton crispus,*
A.madagascariensis, A.ulvaceus,
Barclaya longifolia, Echinodorus
cordifolius, Echinodorus major and
Echinodorus paniculatus.

Deep marginal plants: These plants
grow from bulbs, corms or tubers,
and produce long stems bearing
terminal leaves. Some leaves float on
the surface; others are completely
submerged. Use these plants in the
middleground, background or in the
back corners of the aquarium. The
water lilies *Nymphaea maculata* and
Nymphaea stellata, plus some of the
Aponogetons, can be considered as
deep marginal plants.

Middleground plants: Generally in
the form of rosettes, these plants are
similar to but smaller than specimen
plants. Many Cryptocorynes fit into
this category.

Foreground plants: These small
plants for the front of the tank may be
miniature rosette-forming species,
such as *Cryptocoryne nevillii* and
dwarf varieties of *Cryptocoryne
wendtii* or plants with creeping
rootstocks such as *Lilaeopsis novae-
zelandiae* and *Marsilea crenata*.
Other foreground plants featured in
the species section of the book
include: *Anubias nana, Armoracia
aquatica, Blyxa japonica, Eleocharis
acicularis, Hydrocotyle vulgaris* and
Samolus parviflorus.

Furnishing the tank
Once you are satisfied with the design
of your aquascape and have chosen
the plants to be included, the next
stage is to assemble all the furnishing
materials you will need, such as
gravel, rocks, bogwood plus any
artificial equivalents. It is also
advisable to have some suitable
adhesive available, such as silicone
aquarium sealant, in order to anchor
items firmly in place or build up
structures from smaller pieces.
    First, clean the glass thoroughly
both inside and out, taking particular
care to remove finger marks, dust and
stray fragments of silicone sealant
remaining after manufacture. Next,
blank out the non-viewing sides with

Right: *A selection of simulated rocks
and logs suitable for the aquarium.*
1 *Hollowed tree trunks for hiding
heaters and filters in the corners.*
2 *Curved pieces for terracing.*
3 *A rock cluster with space for a plant
pot.* **4** *A simulated cave, useful as a
territorial or breeding refuge.*
5 *A twisted log with split for planting.*
6 *Small branches to fill odd spaces.*

Below: *A selection of natural
furnishing materials for the aquarium.*
1 *Stratified rock.* **2** *Purple slate.*
3 *Cornish bogwood.* **4** *Brazilian
bogwood.* **5** *Quartz-bearing rock.*
6 *Iron-bearing rock.* **7** *Pebbles of
various size, shape and colour.*
8 *Baked clay aggregate. Be sure to
wash bogwood thoroughly before
use and do not introduce rocks that
may upset the pH value and/or
hardness of the water.*

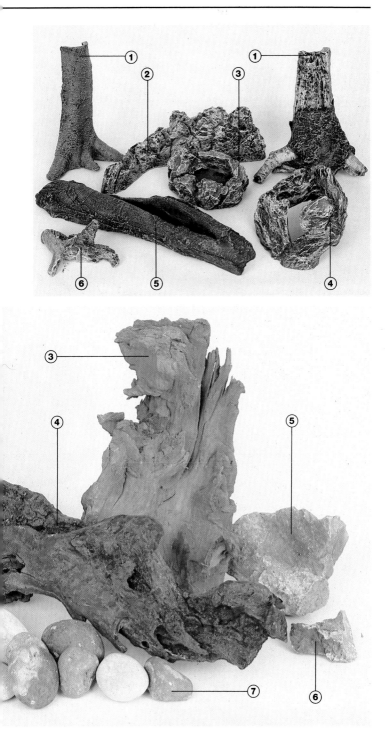

custom-made backing panels or by applying several coats of a suitable emulsion paint to the outside of the tank. In the sequence of four photographs shown on this page the back of the tank has been left uncovered to show up the plants more clearly.

Before adding the gravel, always wash it in running water. Place a quantity of gravel in a bowl and run in water from a hose until the batch is clean. Repeat the process with further batches until all the gravel has been washed. It is surprising how much gravel you need to provide a respectable looking layer. For the minimum ideal depth of 7.5cm (3in) at the back sloping to 5cm (2in) at the front, you will need 6.4 kilos (14lb) of gravel per 900 cm^3 (1ft^2) of floor area.

Before putting the gravel in the tank, you may wish to incorporate a suitable growing medium (see page 28). Also consider the installation of any filtration and/or heating systems (see pages 18-20). Once these arrangements are complete, add the washed gravel carefully to the tank, sloping it as desired.

Planted and left like this, the action of gravity and rooting fishes would soon reduce such a carefully

constructed slope into a uniform plain. To prevent this happening, construct a series of terraces to hold the gravel in position. Fix suitable pieces of rockwork, bogwood or simulated furnishings end to end to create the terrace boundaries. You may need to glue small stones or pebbles into any gaps between odd-shaped pieces.

Once the terracing is complete, install custom-made synthetic pieces to hide filters and heaters, and then add other furnishings to complete the 'artistic' elements of your design. Fill the tank three-quarters full (to prevent spillage when planting) and check that all the electrical apparatus is working. This will include checking that the heater raises the water temperature to the correct level to prevent any thermal shock to tropical plants. The tank is now ready for planting. For safety's sake, always disconnect the electricity supply while you are planting the aquarium.

Planting the aquarium

Check new plants carefully for signs of damage, dying back and unwanted visitors, such as beetles and snails. Rinse the plants in clean water, trim back old brown roots to healthy white tissue using a sharp knife and remove any decaying or yellowing leaves.

Start planting the aquarium at the front, gently pushing rootstocks into the gravel with your fingers and firming the gravel around them. Wrap several rootless cuttings together to form natural looking clumps and

Below: *This is the first photograph in a sequence that demonstrates the usual stages in planting up an aquarium. Here the tank is dry, with the gravel sloped towards the front and terracing built up with simulated furnishings curved for the purpose. The tank used is 75cm (30in) long.*

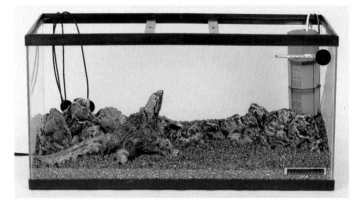

Above: *Synthetic tree trunks hide the tank equipment. The foreground plants include* Cryptocoryne nevillii *(left) and Dwarf Sagittaria (right).*

Below: *Middleground plants include reddish* Rotala macrandra *(centre),* Echinodorus paniculatus *(left centre) and* Aponogeton rigidifolius *(right).*

Below: *The background now begins to take shape, with (left to right)* Vallisneria asiatica, Ludwigia mullertii,

Cabomba caroliniana *and* Synnema triflorum *adding variety of shape to the overall planting in the aquarium.*

insert them into the gravel, having first stripped the lower leaves from the stems. Place pebbles around the base to anchor the cuttings and prevent fishes disturbing them. Plant tubers at an angle of 45°, ensuring that the growing tip is just exposed above the gravel.

Bear in mind that in nature most normally rooted aquatic plants are perennial, but in the aquarium they behave as annuals. After a few months they lose their vitality and become stringy, even when regularly pruned. This is because they are denied the low-water conditions they experience during the dry season in the wild. At this time, most aquatic plants enter their sexual reproductive cycle, producing flowers and then seeds above the water surface. Denied these conditions in the aquarium, they weaken. Tuberous-rooted plants, such as Aponogetons, also need a resting phase in order to retain their vitality. Many plants, however, will grow permanently submerged year after year, increasing

by runners and other vegetative means (see page 49). These species include *Cryptocoryne, Echinodorus, Sagittaria* and *Vallisneria*.

Below: *Simply push rooted plants gently into the aquarium gravel. This technique is demonstrated using an* Echinodorus paniculatus.

Above: *With a printed backdrop behind the tank, the hood fitted and the lights turned on, the planting shapes up as an 'underwater scene'.*

Below: *Insert tubers at an angle of 45°, and leave the growing tip just exposed above the surface. This tuber is* Aponogeton undulatus.

Ecological aquascapes

Attempting to simulate the natural environment of various tropical areas by setting up so-called 'ecological aquascapes' is an increasingly popular pursuit. The characteristics of a tropical rain forest pool, for example, quite clearly differ from those of a rice paddy. It is a question of reproducing the water conditions, temperature, topography, light intensity, plants and fishes of the real situation as closely as possible.

The following areas are ideal environments for such simulations:

Stagnant lowland waters of
   Southeast Asia
Lowland streams of Southeast Asia
Mountain streams of Southeast Asia
Rain forests of South America
Lowland swamps of West Africa

The following descriptions form 'word pictures' of typical situations in these environments (the majority based on the author's experience) and four of them are shown as aquascapes.

Stagnant lowland waters of Southeast Asia

An irrigation canal supplying old overgrown rice paddies near Malacca in western Malaya provides a typical example of this type of environment. The author's observations provide useful insights on which to base an aquarium simulation. 'The water was crystal clear and thickly matted with great clumps of Giant Hygrophila (*Nomaphila stricta*), *Nitella*, *Hydrilla* and water lilies. In the shallows, *Cryptocoryne ciliata* and *Limnocharis* grew in profusion and water lettuce (*Pistia stratiotes*) spread across the surface. The banks were heavily overgrown with palms, bushes and climbers, which cast a dense shade across the surface on one side of the canal. The water temperature was 29°C (84°F); the air temperature 32°C (90°F). Analysis of the water showed a general hardness of 2.4°dH and a pH value of 6.5. The muddy soil was soft and reddish in colour, showing the abundance of iron. Shoals of *Pangasius* catfish could be seen, plus many other fishes, including Striped Barbs and Gouramis.'

Above: *The rain forest bordering a river tributary in Kuantan, eastern Malaya. Here, marginal plants of* *many species grow emersed in the dry season and adapt to growing submersed when the river floods.*

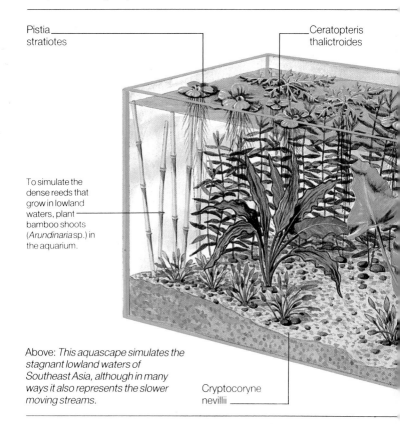

Pistia stratiotes

Ceratopteris thalictroides

To simulate the dense reeds that grow in lowland waters, plant bamboo shoots (*Arundinaria* sp.) in the aquarium.

Above: *This aquascape simulates the stagnant lowland waters of Southeast Asia, although in many ways it also represents the slower moving streams.*

Cryptocoryne nevillii

Above: *A commercial plant collector at work in Southeast Asia, source of many familiar aquarium plants.*

The lowland streams of Southeast Asia

Here, the author examined a small tributary of a river system near Kuantan in eastern Malaya. 'Here again the water was crystal clear, but free of all surface vegetation. *Eleocharis, Limnophila, Blyxa, Cryptocoryne nurri, C.minima* and *Nitella* formed the principal vegetation. The river, its bed strewn with well-rounded pebbles and rocks of reddish hue, was bordered by banks of fine white silver sand on which most of the plants grew. The water hardness was 1°dH and the pH value 5.9. At 11.00am the water temperature was 28°C (82°F). A wealth of fishes swarmed in these waters: Pipefishes, Bumblebee Gobies, Striped Barbs, Coolie Loaches and Red-striped Rasboras were just a few of the species netted in a very short space of time.'

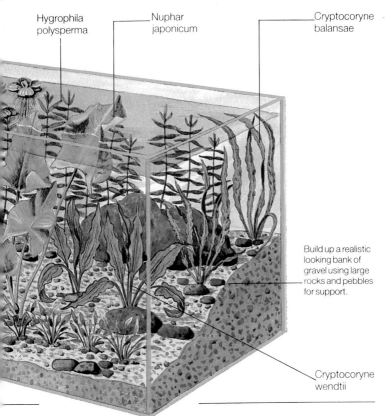

Hygrophila polysperma

Nuphar japonicum

Cryptocoryne balansae

Build up a realistic looking bank of gravel using large rocks and pebbles for support.

Cryptocoryne wendtii

The mountain streams of Southeast Asia

In the Cameron Highlands the author looked at some fast-moving mountain torrents. 'The bed of the stream was composed of jumbled pieces of splintered rock lying between huge rounded boulders. Vegetation was sparse underwater, with just a few unidentified *Cryptocoryne* species managing to maintain a foothold. The water, free of turbulence, was 24°C (75°F) at 9.00am, with a pH value of 5.3 and a general hardness of 2°dH. The banks were heavily clothed with wild bananas, tree ferns and mosses, particularly club mosses and Selaginellas. Loaches darted from rock to rock and large Tinfoil Barbs flashed beneath the surface of the larger pools.'

Use pieces of slate or non-calcareous rock to simulate the rugged terrain.

Aponogeton crispus

Below left and right: *Two mountain streams in Southeast Asia. In fast-moving streams, the bed is scoured clean by the oxygenated water.*

Pieces of bogwood also have a place in this aquascape. Use a single bold branch.

Cryptocoryne affinis

Below: *This aquascape recreates the bed of a mountain stream in S.E. Asia, its sparseness reflecting the 'purging' effects of moving water.*

Vesicularia dubyana

Below: *The rich environment of the Amazon Basin comes alive in this aquascape. There is no shortage of plants to include in this simulation.*

Cabomba piauhyensis

Sagittaria platyphylla

Hydrocotyle vulgaris

The standard grade of aquarium gravel is fine for all these ecological aquascapes. Increase the depth from the 7.5cm (3in) minimum to support large, deep-rooted plants.

Echinodorus tenellus

Hide heaters, filters and other aquarium equipment behind suitable tree roots or simulated furnishings.

The rain forests of South America

With such diverse conditions prevailing over this vast area, it is difficult to generalise. However, in the region of the Amazon and its massive forests the shoreline is submerged during the greater part of the year, the trees standing with their lower trunks and roots beneath the surface. Often, the roots are exposed by the scouring action of the water. The aerial roots of epiphytes trail into the water and produce fine root hairs where they become submerged. The floor consists of debris from the forest above, with rotting logs and a thick layer of decaying leaves overlying the substrate. *Echinodorus* species, both large and small, *Cabomba*,

Myriophyllum, Sagittaria, Bacopa and floating species such as *Salvinia* are typical plants found in this habitat. Fishes such as Angelfishes, *Corydoras, Ancistrus* and *Pimelodella* catfishes, Hatchetfishes, Cardinal and Neon Tetras abound. If Discus Fishes are kept in an ecological aquarium, pairs of dwarf cichlids plus *Corydoras* catfishes could act as companions. A temperature of 27°C (81°F) and a pH value of about 7 should keep both the fishes and plants in good condition.

Right: *In its natural habitat in Peru,* Echinodorus parviflorus *grows both submerged and emersed, an adaptation to changing water levels.*

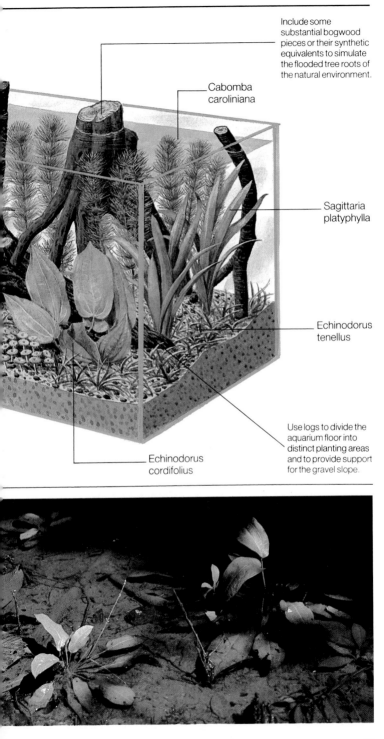

Include some substantial bogwood pieces or their synthetic equivalents to simulate the flooded tree roots of the natural environment.

Cabomba caroliniana

Sagittaria platyphylla

Echinodorus tenellus

Use logs to divide the aquarium floor into distinct planting areas and to provide support for the gravel slope.

Echinodorus cordifolius

43

Lowland swamps of West Africa

The author visited the tiny state of The Gambia on the West coast of Africa, where the rain forests are being destroyed and plants and fishes are adapting to decreasing tree cover. 'One pool was slightly brackish due to the influence of the nearby tidal river. The sandy bottom was thick with debris in the form of rotten logs and the seedpods of various broadleaved evergreen trees that overhung the pool. The water was clear and there were huge clumps of miniature viviparous Blue Water Lilies, Giant Hairgrass (*Eleocharis* sp.), *Marsilea*, *Lagarosiphon* and *Ammannia* species. In a nearby backwater the ground was carpeted with *Anubias* species, with heart-shaped leaves. Small killifishes, *Ctenopoma*, cichlids of the genera *Tilapia* and *Hemichromis*, plus *Synodontis* and other catfishes were the most common species of fish. In the shallows, huge examples of *Ceratopteris* were growing emersed and *Azolla* seemed the most common floating plant. Water temperature was high due to its shallowness, reaching 29°C (84°F) at 8.00am. The pH value was 7.2. The water, slightly brackish to the taste, showed a decidedly brown tinge caused by the presence of humic and tannic acids leaching from falling vegetation.'

Right: *A slow-moving stream in The Gambia in West Africa abounds with aquatic plants, including the floating species* Salvinia *and* Azolla, *plus* Ceratopteris, *growing emersed at the top right-hand corner.*

Below: *The plants and furnishings in this aquarium are intended to simulate a lowland swamp in West Africa, a rich tropical environment.*

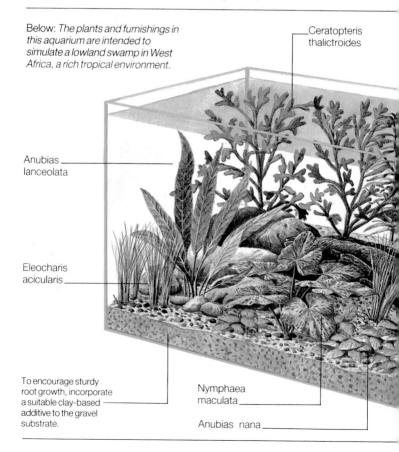

Ceratopteris
thalictroides

Anubias
lanceolata

Eleocharis
acicularis

To encourage sturdy root growth, incorporate a suitable clay-based additive to the gravel substrate.

Nymphaea
maculata

Anubias nana

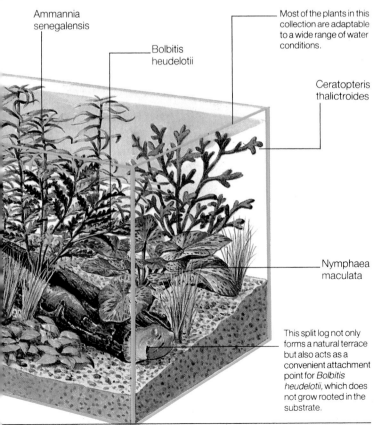

Ammannia
senegalensis

Bolbitis
heudelotii

Most of the plants in this
collection are adaptable
to a wide range of water
conditions.

Ceratopteris
thalictroides

Nymphaea
maculata

This split log not only
forms a natural terrace
but also acts as a
convenient attachment
point for *Bolbitis
heudelotii*, which does
not grow rooted in the
substrate.

Problems with algae

Every aquarium is at some time or other troubled by infestations of algae. What are algae? Where do they come from? How can they be tackled without harming the other plants and the fishes in the aquarium? These are questions that most fishkeepers have asked, perhaps in desperation, at some stage in their lives. Here, we try to provide some answers.

What are algae?
Botanically, algae belong to the division of the plant kingdom known as the Thallophyta, which they share with fungi. Algae are comparatively simple plants that range in form from microscopic unicellular types to gigantic seaweeds that may reach a length of 70m (230ft) in the oceans of the world. Our concern, however, is with the smaller end of this size range.

Important factors contributing to the tenacity and widespread distribution of algae are their incredible reproductive capacity and their ability to survive in a viable state (either in the plant form or as spores) in difficult environments and over long periods of time. Many species of algae can exist in a seemingly desiccated state for many years and their spores can be carried on air currents through the upper atmosphere to encircle the globe. In spite of the heat, cold and radiation, such spores may germinate successfully on their return to a favourable environment after a period of several years.

Although there are species of algae that grow on tree-trunks, on rocks and in damp soil, it is in water that they exist in greatest numbers and variety. Algae have adapted to grow in all types of water: flowing and stagnant; salt and fresh; warm and cold; clean and badly polluted. In the aquarium, they may be found floating on the surface, suspended in the water, or growing in a tangled mass on rocks, plants, gravel or tank equipment. Sometimes, the only indication of their presence is when the water turns green.

The algae most likely to trouble freshwater aquarists fall into the following groups:

Green algae (Chlorophyceae)
Diatoms (Bacillariophyceae)
Whip algae (Euglenophyceae)
Blue-green algae (Myxophyceae)

Let us consider each of these groups.

Green algae This class contains a large proportion of the types encountered in freshwater aquariums. In these algae the green pigment chlorophyll is not masked by other pigments, as it is in other groups.

The unicellular green algae are not visible individually to the naked eye, but appear as a green cloudiness in the water when present in vast numbers. Typical examples are *Chlamydomonas* and *Chlorella*, which forms a green film on the aquarium glass. Multicellular 'colonial' green algae, such as *Volvox*, *Scenedesmus* and *Pandorina*, also cause 'green water'.

The filamentous green algae, in which the individual cells are arranged end to end in long chains, cause frequent problems in aquariums. They may occur as a tangled mass, as in *Spirogyra*, or as green strands attached to rocks and plants, as in *Oedogonium* and *Vaucheria*.

Diatoms Characterized by their silica-impregnated cell walls, diatoms are an important part of the plant plankton that floats in the oceans and in fresh water. Diatoms can proliferate in freshwater aquariums when the levels of phosphate and nitrate are excessively high. They form a brown slime on the gravel, rocks and tank glass, and can even discolour the water in heavy infestations.

Whip algae As their name suggests, the unicellular species in this group have flagellae, or tiny whips, to propel themselves through the water. (In fact, they are on the borders of being classed as unicellular animals, or Protozoa, rather than plants.)

Whip algae rarely cause problems in aquariums because they thrive in such high nitrogen levels that once they begin to proliferate everything else in the tank will have undoubtedly died in the heavily polluted conditions.

Above: *Filamentous green algae can be seen clinging to this pieces of bogwood and spreading across the gravel. A frequent problem in tanks.*

Blue-green algae These organisms share many characteristics of both algae and bacteria, and are now placed in a separate category of their own. In the aquarium they appear as dark green gelatinous sheets that creep over rocks and plants until, unchecked, they can smother everything in the tank. They thrive in bright light and high nitrate and phosphate levels, in both acid and alkaline water. They can produce toxins that are lethal to aquarium fishes.

How do algae reach the aquarium?

In real terms, it is impossible to stop algae reaching the aquarium. As we have seen, the air is filled with algal spores that will germinate on reaching a suitable body of water – including the home aquarium. Algae or algal spores may also be introduced on new plants, snails and even in the faeces of new fishes. Tank furnishings and equipment will also carry algae when moved from one aquarium to another.

The causes of excess algal growth in the aquarium

Once present in the aquarium, algae will grow to excess in fairly well-defined conditions. The most clear-cut cause of excess algal growth is exposure to sunlight; the relative brightness and wide spectral 'richness' of sunlight spur algae to 'bloom' into life.

The same effect occurs, although less markedly, if the artificial illumination in the aquarium is too bright or left on too long. Too low a density of aquarium plants can also allow algae to grow unchecked in the aquarium. And high levels of nitrates, phosphates, sulphates and carbonates act as nutrient 'fuel' to such expansion.

The control of algae

Based on the above causes, the basic strategy for controlling algal growth clearly revolves around the level of light given to the aquarium. But there are many ways in which aquarists can keep algae in check. Try the following useful tips:

1 Ensure that the aquarium is not exposed to sunlight.
2 Install lights of the correct type and power rating.
3 Illuminate the aquarium for only 10 hours a day.
4 Keep the aquarium well planted.
5 Once the underwater plants are thriving, introduce floating aquarium plants to deter the growth of algae. *Ceratophyllum submersum* and *Riccia fluitans* are ideal for this purpose. (See pages 72 and 102.)
6 Inspect all rocks, plants, snails, etc., for algal filaments and sterilize as necessary.
7 Consider introducing algae-grazing fishes, such as *Hypostomus* sp. (Suckermouth Catfishes) and *Gyrenocheilus* sp.
8 Carry out regular partial water changes to keep the level of nitrates, etc, down to acceptable limits.
9 Use a good algicide if none of the above measures has any improvement. Algicides are available mainly as liquid preparations; dose the aquarium water as instructed by the maker. Avoid overdosing.

Propagation

Plants multiply in two basic ways: sexually and asexually. Sexual reproduction involves the production of spores or seeds that germinate to form new plants. Asexual reproduction embraces a number of vegetative processes by which new plants are produced from various parts of the parent plant. Man has harnessed these entirely natural processes, and extended or adapted them in some cases, to develop a number of reliable propagation techniques that can be applied to a wide range of land and water plants. Here we look briefly at the propagation techniques commonly used with aquarium plants.

Sexual propagation techniques

Sexual reproduction in plants relies on the fusion of male and female sex cells, the gametes, to form a zygote. In lower plants, such as algae, mosses, liverworts and ferns, zygotes develop into spores. In the higher plants, such as herbs, shrubs and trees, the zygotes ripen into seeds. In both types of plants, the genetic make-up of new plants is influenced by the characteristics of their respective 'parents'. Thus, only in sexual forms of propagation can change be introduced into succeeding generations.

Man uses this opportunity for variation to the full in horticulture, improving and moulding the characteristics of many plants to suit new conditions or to produce new strains with bolder flowers or heavier crops. In the world of aquarium plants, sexual propagation techniques play a relatively small role compared to the important part played by asexual methods. The lower order plants are seldom propagated by sexual techniques and among the higher plants it is *aquatic* species destined for pool use rather than *aquarium* plants that are reproduced in this way. But since the aim is usually to produce better and more colourful blooms – a factor which has no bearing on aquarium culture – it is easy to see why comparatively little experimentation has been attempted with the majority of aquarium plants.

Above: *The lovely flower spike of* Aponogeton longiplumulosus *unfurls above the surface. The seeds that form germinate readily in the gravel.*

Nevertheless, there are certain aquarium plants that can be usefully propagated by sexual techniques. In order to produce seeds, the plants must first produce flowers. And here we can make a reasonable distinction between aquarium plants that readily produce flowers and those that need a little coaxing.

In the first group we can include deep marginals, such as species of *Aponogeton* and the water lilies (the latter suitable in aquariums only as young plants), that grow from a rootstock embedded in the bottom soil. These plants produce leaves and flowers that float on the surface. Pollinated largely by insects, the flowers set seeds and these germinate readily in the substrate.

Most aquatic plants fall into the second category. These were once land-living species that have colonized water relatively recently in evolutionary terms. They still retain their ancestral habit of producing flowers and seeds, but only when the water level falls low enough for them to grow emersed. Therefore it is unlikely that these plants will flower constantly submerged in an aquarium. In this group we can include most Cryptocorynes and species of *Echinodorus, Hygrophila* and *Ludwigia.*

With perhaps only half a dozen species is seed the regular mode of production on a commercial basis.

These include *Samolus parviflorus*, *Echinodorus berteroi* and *Ludwigia* sp. The technique used under greenhouse conditions is as follows. The level of the water in which the plants are growing submersed is gradually allowed to fall. This stimulates the plants to produce stiffer aerial leaves and then flowering shoots. Leaving the vents open in the greenhouse allows insects to cross pollinate the flowers in a totally natural way. The ripe seed is then collected and sprinkled over the surface of shallow pans of sowing compost. Normally, seeds germinate quickly, but in some species germination may be delayed for several weeks or even months. The soil in the pans is kept just moist until the seedlings have

Below: *This specimen of* Limnophila aquatica *shows a clear distinction between the submersed and emersed growth. The firm aerial shoots make ideal cuttings.*

reached at least 10cm (4in) or so high. The pan is then flooded with water and soon after the plants transferred to their permanent quarters.

This technique can be used in the aquarium where the opportunity exists. As an alternative to insect pollination of the flowers, use a fine paint brush to transfer pollen from the stamens to the stigmas. Do remember that the resulting seeds have no storage life at all and must be sown immediately.

Asexual propagation techniques
Asexual techniques are widely used in commerce and in the hobby for reproducing aquarium plants. The methods involved range from simple division to the complex realms of tissue culture, although the latter is strictly a commercial process. Here we review these methods.

Runners Most aquarium plants produce outgrowths called runners. These elongated shoots arise from leaf axils (i.e. the junction of a leaf and the stem) on the side shoots, but occasionally from the apical shoot. They either run along the surface of the substrate, as in *Vallisneria* sp. and *Echinodorus tenellus*, or grow underground for a while before pushing up to the surface, as in the Cryptocorynes. A baby plant, usually called a slip, develops at the tip of each runner. When this has put roots down into the substrate and become established, it also produces one or more runners. And so the aquarium quickly becomes colonized by new plants in this way.

It is best to allow each baby plant to develop undisturbed for a time and to reach a few centimetres in height before detaching it from the parent plant. While they can be detached earlier without harm, this may prevent such baby plants from producing runners successfully when they mature. Left to themselves, the connections between the parent and baby plants eventually break down.

Some floating plants, such as *Limnobium laevigatum* and *Pistia stratiotes*, also spread rapidly in this way. Each plant produces several runners at the same time.

Above: *The elongated creeping shoots of* Hydrocotyle leucocephala *produce roots at each node. Simply separate each rooted section.*

Below: *A daughter plant (a 'slip') produced at the tip of a runner is clearly visible in this specimen of* Sagittaria platyphylla.

Offsets These are new plants produced on outgrowths that are similar to runners but shorter and stouter. Many species of *Echinodorus* gradually form large clumps by continually producing offsets. To propagate such plants, simply divide the clump into smaller plants and set these in the substrate.

Rhizomes Rhizomes are underground stems that superficially appear rootlike, but can be identified as stems by the presence of scalelike leaves and buds. They serve not only as food storage organs to tide plants over during dormant periods but also as a natural means of asexual reproduction.

Many aquatic plants grow from rhizomes. These include *Acorus gramineus*, *Nuphar* sp. and *Nymphaea* sp. To propagate these plants, simply cut or split the rhizome into pieces and each piece will develop new shoots and roots. In some plants, the rhizome branches freely and thus is ideal for propagation in this way. Conversely, certain species of *Aponogeton* grow from a storage organ – called a tuber – that scarcely branches at all and has just one growing tip. Cutting this to try and propagate it will kill the plant.

Above: *A portion of* Houttuynia cordata *showing the underground runner giving rise to a new plant. This species spreads rapidly.*

Above: *The simplest way of gaining new plants of* Samolus parviflorus *is to gently pull apart the rosette and plant the pieces separately.*

Below: *A pair of adventitious plantlets developing on a flowering stem of* Echinodorus parviflorus. *1 Flowering stem of parent plant 2 Plantlets arising at nodes 3 Fully developed, functional roots.*

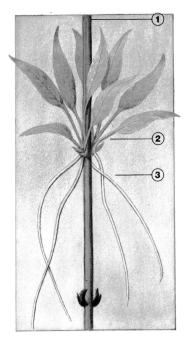

Adventitious shoots As the name suggests, these are plantlets that arise from any organ of the mother plant. There are countless examples of adventitious shoots developing on aquarium plants. The floating form of the Indian Fern, *Ceratopteris thalictroides*, produces hundreds of tiny ferns at the leaf margins. Eventually, these detach and float away to grow independently. Plantlets also develop on older leaves of submerged specimens. Java Fern, *Microsorium pteropus*, develops into large colonies by reproducing itself in the same way. In this case, the young plants attach their roots to stones or bark close to the mother plant.

Nymphaea daubenyana, a water lily from West Africa, produces tiny water lilies from the centre of the floating pads. *Eleocharis vivipara* produces new plants on the tips of the leaves. In emerse-grown plants, the tips naturally bend over and enable the plantlets to put out roots where they touch the ground. Thus, vast colonies of this plant are formed in a very short period of time. If left unseparated on submerged specimens, several tiers of rosettes may develop one on top of another.

Adventitious plantlets are produced on the flowering stems of

51

many aquarium plants, including certain species of *Echinodorus*, such as *E.cordifolius, E.paniculatus* and *E.parviflorus*. Simply peg these stems down and separate the plantlets when about 15cm (6in) high.

Cuttings Taking cuttings is a familiar technique for propagating many houseplants and garden plants. In many ways, taking cuttings of aquarium plants is even easier. Cuttings taken from land plants are in danger of drying out before roots are formed; being constantly bathed in water, cuttings of aquarium plants are not at risk in this way. In fact, the vast majority of aquarium plants supplied by retail outlets are in the form of top cuttings, i.e. taken from the top section of the plant, including the growing tip.

Cuttings can also be taken from side shoots and from middle portions of the plants. And, of course, the original part of the plant remaining after the cuttings have been taken will usually sprout again. In most species, roots form only at the nodes. In some plants, however, such as *Nomaphila stricta*, internodal roots are produced in great abundance.

Take cuttings using a sharp knife or secateurs, or merely tear away a suitable side shoot with a piece of

Above: *Taking a top cutting of* Telanthera lilacina, *one of many aquarium plants that are easily propagated in this way.*

Below: *The basal portion of a* Limnophila aquatica *begins to produce healthy new shoots after the top section has been removed.*

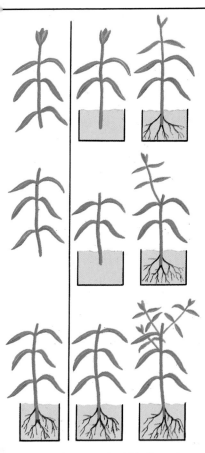

Top cuttings

Since it contains the active growing point, the top section of a plant usually makes a very reliable cuttings. Once separated, simply remove the lower leaves from the cutting and insert the severed end in the gravel. Roots will develop and the shoot should grow away strongly.

Middle shoot cuttings

Although it will take longer to establish, the middle portion of a plant will normally succeed as a cutting. Success depends not only on roots developing but also on the emergence of a side shoot from the axil of a leaf. If grown emersed, dip the cut end in a hormone rooting preparation to speed rooting.

Basal portion

No part of a plant is wasted when cuttings are taken. Left undisturbed, the basal portion should produce side shoots from buds in the leaf axils. These will become the new growing points and will create a bushier plant, the principle on which pruning for shape is based. Many aquarium plants benefit from being pruned to keep their growth in check.

nodal tissue attached. Ideally, each cutting should have two or three nodes, although even single nodes can succeed. If the cuttings are to be grown emerse, remove the lower leaves and dip the base in a fungicide to prevent 'damping off'. Dipping the cutting into hormone rooting powder will help roots to form more quickly. Insert the lower third of the each cutting into moist growing medium and keep them in humid conditions.

Many plants, such as *Egeria* sp., *Myriophyllum* sp., *Ludwigia* sp. etc, will produce new roots if stem cuttings are simply left to float in the aquarium water. Once roots have formed, insert them into the gravel and anchor them securely until the roots take a good hold. Cuttings may also be taken from leaves, as in *Synnema triflorum*, or even from pieces of rootstock in other species.

Tissue culture This is a well-established technique for the rapid multiplication of disease-free stock of trees, shrubs and herbaceous plants. It is also used where the amount of plant material available is limited, as in a new or rare species. Its current experimental use for aquarium plants centres around those species – certain Cryptocorynes, for example – that increase only slowly by other methods. Basically, it involves taking minute amounts of tissue from a plant and culturing it on nutrient jelly under strictly controlled sterile conditions. Thousands of plants can be produced in this way in a very short time. It is a very expensive process to set up, however, and is strictly a commercial endeavour that will be applied only to rare and expensive subjects, such as hybrid water lilies, for the forseeable future.

Classification of plants

Why do plants have scientific names? What is wrong with the common names? The problem is that a common name may be understood in only a small area. As an example, a marsh plant with a scientific name of *Chlorophytum bichetii* has been offered in commerce under the following names: Ivory Rush, Wheat Plant, Chinese Medicine Plant, Chinese Temple Plant and Striped Rush. This is very confusing, especially since at least one of the common names is also applied to another species of aquatic plant. But there is really only one plant called *Chlorophytum bichetii*.

Thus, scientific names avoid confusion. But they do much more than that because they also classify plants in terms of their characteristics and how they relate to other plants.

How taxonomy works

The fundamental principles of classifying living things, known as taxonomy, were crystallized in the 1750s by the Swedish botanist Linnaeus. It was Linnaeus who devised the system of using two names, the genus and species, to 'label' each living organism in Latin for future reference. This basic system, so-called binominal nomenclature, has survived the centuries and is still the universal system recognized throughout the world.

To appreciate how aquarium plants are classified, it is sufficient to understand that two or more plants that share the same genetical make-up – but that are not necessarily exactly identical – are grouped together as a species. In our example, '*bichetii*' is the specific name or epithet of the plant. At the next level of classification, plants with some differences but with sufficient characteristics in common to show that they were derived from the same evolutionary stock are placed together in a grouping known as a genus. Thus, '*Chlorophytum*' is the generic name of our example.

And so the classification continues into ever wider, more embracing

---

A selection of specific epithets and their meanings

acicularis	sharply pointed, like a needle
affinis	related to
albida	whitish
amazonicus	growing in the Amazon region
aquatica, -cum, -lis	living in water
auriculata	with ear-like appendages
balansae	named after the French botanist Balansa
blassii	named after the German importer Blass
boivinianus	named after the Canadian botanist Boivin
caroliniana	from Carolina, North America
ciliata	fringed, as if with cilia
cordata	heart-shaped
cordifolius	with heart-shaped leaves
costata	ribbed
crenata	with rounded teeth
crispus	crisp
densus	dense
diandra	with two stamens
difformis	differently formed
dubyana	named after the Swiss botanist Duby
fluitans	floating, swimming
graminea, -us	grasslike

groupings. A group of similar genera is called a family and a group of similar families is an order. Such classification is based not only on the outward appearance of each plant, including the flower structure, but also on biochemical and physiological considerations.

Classifying plants into convenient 'boxes' enables us to make useful assumptions about plants new to us that share that particular box. Thus, if we are familiar with *Echinodorus* species in general then we can assume that an unfamiliar *Echinodorus* species will share certain characteristics, such as basic shape and growing requirements.

The only cloud on such a simplistic horizon is that many plants – and aquarium plants are no exception – are classified to even finer degrees than species. Thus, hybrid names, varieties, subspecies, cultivars, credits to individual botanists, etc, appear to clutter and confuse once simple and elegant scientific names. And as a further and continuing complication, scientific names are constantly being updated and changed according to international standards and codes.

At the other end of this spiralling hierarchy of nomenclature lie the plants themselves and the commercial growers and importers who supply them to hobbyists the world over. At this, the 'business' end of the market, the scientific names for many plants have become so familiar as 'trade' names that they continue to be used in spite of the latest round of reclassification by more theoretical plant lovers. Thus, in the species part of this book, you will find the plants presented in A-Z order of the scientific names acknowledged in horticultural circles, rather than in strictly botanical ones.

As a guide to the seemingly complex world of scientific names, we include a table of selected specific epithets and their literal translation or derivation. Many reflect the plant's shape; others show the geographical origin or acknowledge a botanist.

minima	very small
nana	dwarflike
nevillii	named after the discoverer of the plant Nevill
parviflorus	with small flowers
platyphylla	with broad leaves
polysperma	bearing many seeds
pteropus	with a winged stem
retrospiralis	coiling backwards
senegalensis	growing in Senegal
spiralis	coiled
stellata	star-shaped
stratiotes	sword-shaped
submersum	submerged
subulata	slender and tapering to a point
tenellus	tender, soft
thaianum	growing in Thailand
thalictroides	resembling the meadow-rue *Thalictrum*
thwaitesii	named after the British botanist Thwaites
tortifolia	with twisted leaves
ulvaceus	resembling the marine alga *Ulva*
undulatus	wavy
vulgaris	common, ordinary
walkeri	named after the North American botanist Walker
wendtii	named after the German aquarist Wendt
zosterifolia	with leaves resembling the eelgrass *Zostera*

Species section

Aquatic plants embrace thousands of species. Many of those suitable for aquarium use are imported from the wild or grown in specialist nurseries that supply the hobby. Many other species remain undiscovered or have yet to be collected from areas that are inaccessible for geographical or political reasons.

This section of the book features a representative selection of 68 species, plus references to similar species of interest. The plants are presented in alphabetical order of their most familiar scientific name – usually the one by which they are known to plant dealers – followed by any relevant common names. The text entries are intended to give a clear and concise description of each plant so that the aquarist can easily choose suitable species for any particular aquarium or location. The reference value of the text is further enhanced by the five-point summary of environmental conditions in which each species will thrive.

All the plants included in this section are readily available and are capable of being grown under normal aquarium conditions. Really difficult species have been excluded, as have certain marsh and bog plants that, although frequently offered for sale, have a limited life when submerged in aquariums. In fact, it is surprising how many totally unsuitable plants – often simply houseplants – are incorrectly offered as aquarium plants.

When choosing plants for a new aquarium, select a few carefully considered types. This will avoid setting up a 'museum collection' of individual specimens of many different species arranged haphazardly in the tank. When buying plants, avoid those stored in dark, cold situations that may have shed their lower leaves or show signs of decay or brown spots. It is very difficult to revive a plant that has received such a severe check on its growth.

Descriptive terms used in the species section

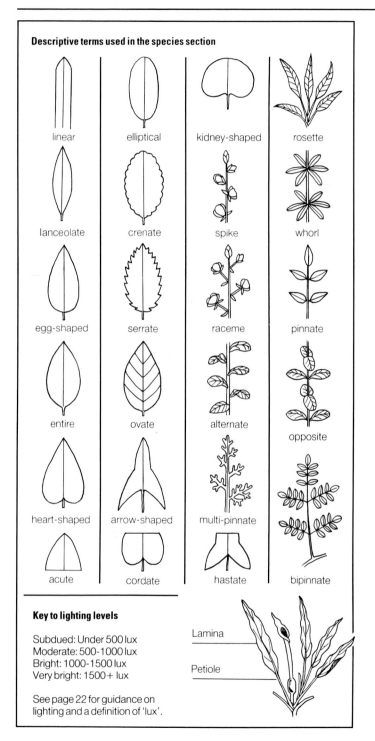

linear

elliptical

kidney-shaped

rosette

lanceolate

crenate

spike

whorl

egg-shaped

serrate

raceme

pinnate

entire

ovate

alternate

opposite

heart-shaped

arrow-shaped

multi-pinnate

acute

cordate

hastate

bipinnate

Key to lighting levels

Subdued: Under 500 lux
Moderate: 500-1000 lux
Bright: 1000-1500 lux
Very bright: 1500+ lux

See page 22 for guidance on
lighting and a definition of 'lux'.

Lamina

Petiole

Acorus gramineus
Japanese Rush
- **Substrate:** Plain washed gravel
- **Lighting:** Not critical
- **pH value:** 6.8-7.5
- **Hardness:** Not critical
- **Temperature:** 15-21°C (59-70°F)

Height: Up to 30cm (12in).
Distribution: Eastern Asia.
Characteristics: A slow-growing plant with handsome dark green spiky leaves in fan-shaped clumps. The roots are very tough and wiry.
Aquarium use: This moisture-loving plant is suitable for growing submerged in the aquarium. It thrives at the lower end of the recommended temperature range but does reasonably well in tropical aquariums.
Propagation: Divide the plants by splitting the rhizome.
Varieties: Although the type species is available, the following varieties are more extensively cultivated: *Acorus gramineus* var. *variegatus*, which grows to the same height as the type species but with leaves strikingly striped in yellow. *Acorus gramineus* var. *pussilus*, a dwarf form that grows up to 10cm (4in) high and is suitable for foreground planting. *Acorus gramineus* var. *intermedius*, a robust form reaching 45cm (18in) high.

Below: **Aglaonema simplex**
This jungle bog plant will stand submersion for long periods.

Above: **Acorus gramineus**
An excellent middleground plant for both cool and tropical aquariums.

Aglaonema simplex
Malayan Sword; Borneo Sword
- **Substrate:** Plain washed gravel
- **Lighting:** Moderate
- **pH value:** Not critical
- **Hardness:** Not critical
- **Temperature:** 23°C (73°F)

Height: Up to 38cm (15in).
Distribution: Malaysia.
Characteristics: The leaves, reddish when young and mid to dark green and often glossy when mature, are broadly ovate with bluntly pointed tips. Malayan Sword grows from a creeping rootstock and develops fairly slowly in the aquarium. Although

it will reach 38cm (15in) eventually, it is imported at much smaller sizes.
Aquarium use: Middleground.
Propagation: By division of the rhizome, which is practical only when the plant is grown emerse.

Alternanthera rosaefolia
Red Hygrophila
- **Substrate:** Plain washed gravel
- **Lighting:** Very bright
- **pH value:** Not critical
- **Hardness:** Not critical
- **Temperature:** 18-20°C (64-68°F)

Height: Up to 50cm (20in).
Distribution: Widely distributed in tropical regions.
Characteristics: An extremely attractive plant, with the deepest red coloration of any aquatic species. The lanceolate leaves, up to 7.5cm (3in) long and 1.25cm (0.5in) wide, are carried on multibranched woody stems. Their colour varies from dark wine-red to pink, with the undersurface and stems similarly coloured.
Aquarium use: Middleground to background. A difficult species to grow successfully, it requires very strong light to thrive. Do not crowd the plant or it will shed the lower leaves due to lack of light. Plant in bunches of four to six stems. It may also be grown emersed but is very prone to attack by red spider.
Propagation: Take cuttings up to 25cm (10in) long, remove the lower two pairs of leaves and insert the cuttings at least 5cm (2in) into the aquarium gravel.
Other species: Other species are available but they do not respond as well to submersion as *A.rosaefolia*. See also *Telanthera lilacina*, described on page 110.

Ammannia senegalensis
Red Ammannia
- **Substrate:** Plain washed gravel
- **Lighting:** Very bright
- **pH value:** Not critical
- **Hardness:** Not critical
- **Temperature:** 20-26°C (68-79°F)

Height: Up to 45cm (18in), but normally smaller.
Distribution: Tropical and subtropical Africa.
Characteristics: A herbaceous plant with erect and prostrate growth patterns, depending on the water level. The leaves are elliptical to lanceolate, up to 3cm (1.2in) long by 1cm (0.4in) wide and pale green to

Below: **Alternanthera rosaefolia**
A striking aquarium subject that thrives in really bright conditions.

Above: **Ammannia senegalensis**
The colour of the leaves varies with the light intensity. Here, bright lighting causes a pink tinge in the plants.

olive-brown or pale red in colour, depending on the light intensity.
Aquarium use: Background bunch plant. An impressive subject that does well in the recommended temperature range. It needs a great deal of light to thrive. Ideally, plant this species at the rear of the aquarium in bunches of five or six cuttings. This plant may prove difficult and further investigation is needed to establish the correct technique for growing it successfully in a submerged state.

Propagation: Take cuttings 15-20cm (6-8in) long and remove the lower two pairs of leaves. It is also possible to grow Red Ammannia from seeds, which are freely produced when the plant is grown emersed. Sow the ripe seeds in shallow pans and gradually raise the water level as the seedlings develop.

Other species: Other species of *Ammannia* are often imported but difficulty in identifying them is leading to some confusion.

Below: **Ammannia senegalensis**
Amid other aquarium plants, the olive-brown leaves provide a pleasing contrast to various shades of green.

Anubias nana

Dwarf Anubias
- **Substrate:** Rich
- **Lighting:** Subdued
- **pH value:** Not critical
- **Hardness:** Not critical
- **Temperature:** 25°C (77°F)

Height: 15cm (6in).
Distribution: Tropical West Africa.
Characteristics: This pretty little plant is the pygmy of the family. The dark green elliptical to egg-shaped leaves are borne on short petioles that arise from a creeping stem. It flowers frequently when grown emersed, producing a spathe typical of the Aroid group to which it belongs.
Aquarium use: Foreground plant. Although rarely found growing submersed in nature, this plant adapts readily to aquarium conditions.
Propagation: By division of the fairly thick rhizome.
Other species: *Anubias afzelii* from Sierra Leone, which reaches a height of 38cm (15in) with dark green lanceolate leaves. *Anubias barteri* from Nigeria and the Cameroons reaches 30cm (12in) and has hastate leaves borne on stems of greater length. A most attractive plant.

Above: **Anubias nana**
Plant this dainty species in natural looking clumps at the front of the aquarium. It is very tolerant of changes in the pH value and mineral content of the water, but does prefer a substrate rich in nutrients.

Aponogeton boivinianus
- **Substrate:** Full of nutrients
- **Lighting:** Not critical
- **pH value:** Around 7.5
- **Hardness:** Not critical
- **Temperature:** 18-25°C (64-77°F)

Height: Up to 75cm (30in) in well-grown specimens.
Distribution: Northern Madagascar.
Characteristics: This plant grows permanently submerged. The round flattened tuber produces a rosette of broad, elongated dark green leaves with a highly indented surface. The leaf tips are blunt or slightly acute. The stems may be up to 45cm (18in) long.
Aquarium use: Background or middleground specimen plant. Contrary to other reports, the author has found this an easy plant to grow and very long lasting in the aquarium. It will thrive in slightly alkaline water and, like all Aponogetons, requires ample feeding in order to build up

food stores on which to draw during the next growing cycle.

Propagation: This has not been achieved so far. Supplies rely on freshly imported tubers.

Aponogeton crispus
Wavy-edged Swordplant
- ● **Substrate:** Rich with nutrients
- ● **Lighting:** Not critical
- ● **pH value:** Not critical
- ● **Hardness:** Not critical
- ● **Temperature:** 20-25°C (68-77°F)

Height: Usually up to 45cm (18in), but sometimes larger.

Distribution: Southeast Asia, especially Sri Lanka.

Characteristics: The plant produces a basal rosette of submerged leaves with either short or long leaf stalks (petioles), depending on the lighting. (Longer petioles develop in dimmer conditions.) The leaves are variable but they are normally broadly lanceolate with

Below: **Aponogeton boivinianus**
Rooted in a substrate well supplied with nutrients, this impressive plant will thrive in tropical aquariums. Ideal as a single specimen plant.

pointed tips and wavy edges. Floating leaves are rarely produced by cultivated plants; if they do develop this often indicates that the plant is a hybrid with other Sri Lankan species that occur very commonly in the wild.
Aquarium use: Middleground specimen plant, ideal for planting at the sides of the aquarium. It is an undemanding species that thrives in the recommended temperature range, although rich substrate with added fertilizer is needed to maintain vigour. After growing strongly for 6-9 months, the plant sheds the larger leaves, retaining only the smaller basal ones. At this point, remove the plants from the aquarium and store them in cooler water at about 10°C (50°F). After a period of about two months, replace the plants in the main aquarium and they should grow away strongly again.
Propagation: Seeds freely produced from the single white inflorescence fall to the bottom of the aquarium, germinate in the substrate and grow away quite freely.

Below: **Aponogeton crispus**
The wavy-edged leaves of this undemanding plant provide a bold accent in the aquarium. Be sure to rest the tuber for about two months in cooler water when leaves are shed.

Aponogeton madagascariensis

Laceleaf Plant; Madagascar Laceplant

- **Substrate:** Plain washed gravel
- **Lighting:** Moderate
- **pH value:** Not critical
- **Hardness:** Not critical
- **Temperature:** 15-25°C (59-77°F)

Height: Up to 75cm (30in).
Distribution: Originally Madagascar, but it has been introduced to Mauritius, where it is quite common.
Characteristics: The tuber, up to 12.5cm (5in) long and often branched, produces a rosette of submerged leaves up to 50cm (20in) long. The petioles take up about half this length and support leaf blades (laminae) of long elliptical shape about 8cm (3.2in) wide. The most striking feature of these mid to dark green or brown-green leaves is that they are skeletonized. Although seemingly delicate, they are really quite tough.
Aquarium use: Specimen middleground plant. Indifferent to water chemistry, the newly imported tubers sprout readily and grow strongly to produce beautiful plants. Subsequently, the plants die down and the tuber seems unable to build up sufficient nutrients for the next growth cycle, and generally disintegrates. Much experimentation needs to be done before these Madagascan Aponogetons can be maintained reliably from year to year. Even so, these plants make a fine, if

Above:
Aponogeton madagascariensis
These extraordinary specimen plants sprout readily from imported tubers.

temporary, aquarium display
Propagation: Divide the newly imported tubers. Although the plant does produce seeds in the aquarium, they seldom germinate and if they do the seedlings soon perish.

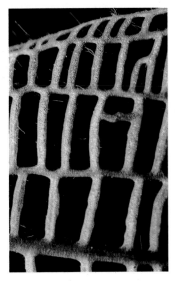

Above:
Aponogeton madagascariensis
The fascinating skeletonized leaves are much stronger than they appear. Other species have similar leaves.

Aponogeton ulvaceus
- **Substrate:** Plain washed gravel
- **Lighting:** Not critical
- **pH value:** Around 7.5
- **Hardness:** Not critical
- **Temperature:** 22°C (72°F)

Height: Up to 60cm (24in).
Distribution: Central and northern Madagascar.
Characteristics: A permanently submerged aquatic plant that in nature grows in both still and flowing waters and in both shady and sunlit situations. The large leaves – up to 30cm (12in) long and 8cm (3in) wide – are borne on petioles of equal length. The pale green laminae are undulate and slightly translucent, and may develop a reddish tinge in strong light. The leaves arise from a cone-shaped, slightly hairy tuber. *Note*: Plants offered from Sri Lanka under this name are always a native species.
Aquarium use: Specimen middleground plant. This is the easiest of the Madagascan Aponogetons to cultivate. Although indifferent to water chemistry, it seems to prefer slightly alkaline conditions and thrives at slightly lower temperatures of about 22°C (72°F). It flowers freely, the twin-forked yellow inflorescences often producing seeds that germinate freely in the aquarium. The plant overwinters well at a temperature of 12°C (54°F). It is very vulnerable to attack by snails, however, and these must be

Above: **Aponogeton ulvaceus**
A very adaptable specimen plant that flowers readily in the aquarium.

rigorously eliminated from the tank.
Propagation: By seeds.
Other species: *A.longiplumulosus* from northwestern Madagascar, a large easily cultivated species. *A.henkelianus*, similar to the Laceleaf Plant but the leaves are not so finely skeletonized.

Aponogeton undulatus
- **Substrate:** Plain washed gravel
- **Lighting:** Not critical
- **pH value:** 6.8-7.2
- **Hardness:** 10-15°dH
- **Temperature:** 20°C (68°F) minimum

Height: 30cm (12in).
Distribution: Sri Lanka, India.
Characteristics: The tuberous rootstock is ovoid, about 5cm (2in) long and 2.5cm (1in) in diameter in large specimens. The pale green elliptical leaves – 10-15cm (4-6in) long with gently undulating margins – are supported by petioles about 15cm (6in) in length. White flowers are borne on a single spike. Floating leaves are never produced; if they are, the plant is either a hybrid or has been confused with the similar species *A.natans*. Note: *A.stachyosporus*, which comes from Malaya and Thailand, is considered to be the true *A.undulatus* by some authorities. This

plant has transparent panels on the leaves and also produces viviparous plantlets on the flower spikes.

Aquarium use: Middleground plant. It thrives in mildly acid to slightly alkaline conditions and can tolerate slightly lower heat levels than those suggested by the minimum recommended temperature. Like other Asian Aponogetons with a tuberous rootstock, it should be rested in cool water.

Propagation: By seeds sown in shallow water. Viviparous plantlets in *A.stachyosporus* are formed on a potential flower stem that fails to reach the surface. Bend the stem over and peg it down to the gravel with lead wire, enabling the baby plants to root in the gravel. When they are 7.5-10cm (3-4in) high, separate these developing plants from the parent and establish them elsewhere in the aquarium.

Other species: Other Asian Aponogetons imported include *A.rigidifolius*, a most attractive plant

Below: **Aponogeton undulatus**
The pale green leaves provide a refreshing contrast to darker plants.

Above: **Armoracia aquatica**
This easy-to-grow foreground plant bears white flowers on aerial stems.

with a long creeping rootstock rather than a tuber. It is rather more demanding in cultivation.

Armoracia aquatica
(Also known as Rorippa aquatica)
American Cress
- ● **Substrate:** Plain washed gravel
- ● **Lighting:** Bright
- ● **pH value:** Not critical
- ● **Hardness:** Not critical
- ● **Temperature:** 18-25°C (64-77°F)

Height: Up to 8cm (3.2in) in the submerged form, but flowering spikes may reach 25cm (10in) high.
Distribution: Eastern North America.
Characteristics: The basic form of the plant is a rosette with submerged brittle leaves that vary in shape from elliptical leaves without a petiole to highly divided, almost fernlike foliage. The aerial leaves produced are less brittle and entire. White flowers form but seldom produce viable seed.
Aquarium use: An adaptable plant suitable as a foreground subject in both temperate and tropical aquariums. It tolerates a wide range of pH and °dH values, and although it prefers a well-lit position it will adapt to shadier conditions.
Propagation: By cuttings of aerial shoots or by leaf cuttings taken from the base of the plant.

67

Bacopa caroliniana

Giant Red Bacopa
- **Substrate:** Plain washed gravel
- **Lighting:** Not critical
- **pH value:** 6.8-7.2
- **Hardness:** 10-15°dH
- **Temperature:** 18-24°C (64-75°F)

Height: Up to 30cm (12in) when submerged, but only half this when grown emersed.

Distribution: Florida northwards to Virginia, eastern USA.

Characteristics: A water-loving bog plant that submerges well. The thick fleshy stems bear opposite, oval, pale green leaves that turn a rich coppery red in bright light. Blue flowers are borne in the axils of emerse-grown plants.

Aquarium use: A middleground to background plant, depending on the height of the tank. Plant in bunches of four to five stems, after first removing the lower two sets of leaves.

Propagation: Take cuttings about 12.5-25cm (5-10in) long.

Other species: These include *B.monnieri*, similar but smaller in all respects. *B.amplexicaulis*, which is larger than *B.caroliniana* but does not stand prolonged submersion. There is a variegated form of this species. *B.myriophiloides* is an attractive little plant with thin stems that bear whorls of short, pale to mid green leaves.

Barclaya longifolia

Orchid Lily
- **Substrate:** Rich, lime free
- **Lighting:** Not critical
- **pH value:** 6.8-7.2
- **Hardness:** 4-6°dH
- **Temperature:** 25-30° (77-86°F)

Height: Up to 35cm (14in).

Distribution: Malaya, Thailand and Burma.

Characteristics: This member of the Water Lily Family, or Nymphaeaceae, is one of the most

Below: **Bacopa caroliniana**
An extremely useful plant for filling out the middle, back or corners of the aquarium. At home in hard water and easy to propagate from cuttings.

beautiful of aquarium plants and consequently in great demand. Once rare, supplies are now plentiful. The plant grows from a tuberous rhizome, producing a rosette of lanceolate leaves with undulating margins and borne on short petioles. The upper leaf surface is glossy green or brown; the undersurface, a deep reddish purple. Vigorous plants may produce orchid-like flowers – hence the common name. They often produce viable seed.

Aquarium use: Centrepiece middleground plant.

Propagation: By seeds, sown when fresh. (Do not store seeds dry.)

Bolbitis heudelotii
African Water Fern
- **Substrate:** Not applicable
- **Lighting:** Subdued
- **pH value:** Not critical
- **Hardness:** 3-18°dH
- **Temperature:** 22-28°C (72-82°F)

Height: About 25-38cm (10-15in) when submerged, but much larger in emersed specimens.

Above: **Barclaya longifolia**
To encourage the full beauty of the Orchid Lily, grow this decorative plant in a large warm aquarium with a rich, lime-free substrate and fairly soft water. An ideal centrepiece.

Distribution: Tropical West Africa

Characteristics: This fern of the Family Polypodiaceae has a dark green to black creeping rhizome covered in short black scales. Black wiry shoots anchor the rhizome to hard surfaces. The stalked leaves are dark green and multipinnate, up to 30cm (12in) long.

Aquarium use: For decorating pieces of bogwood and rockwork. Attach it by means of rubber bands; this plant will not grow in the gravel. It demands clear, soft to medium-hard water and seems to do best if placed near to the outflow of a power filter. Not an easy plant.

Propagation: By cuttings of the creeping rhizome. Preferably, choose pieces with a growing shoot. Middle cuttings will succeed, although they will take rather longer to establish.

69

Above: **Bolbitis heudelotii**
A tropical fern that thrives in subdued lighting conditions. Attach it to rocks and bogwood in the tank.

Top right: **Blyxa japonica**
An effective foreground plant that lives in still or slowly moving waters throughout Southeast Asia.

Blyxa japonica
Bamboo Plant
- **Substrate:** Rich in mulm (detritus)
- **Lighting:** Moderate
- **pH value:** 7.0
- **Hardness:** Not critical
- **Temperature:** 25°C (77°F)

Height: 15cm (6in).
Distribution: Widely distributed in Southeast Asia.
Characteristics: A bushy plant with linear, sharply pointed leaves of grey-green carried on ascending stems. Flowers, white and borne terminally on thin stems, are often found on imported plants. This species is said to be an annual, but constant propagation of the side shoots keeps the plant growing continuously.
Aquarium use: Foreground plant.
Propagation: Pull the side shoots away gently and plant them separately in the aquarium gravel.

Below: Cabomba caroliniana
The finely divided leaves soon attract floating debris and so good filtration is essential in the aquarium.

Cabomba caroliniana

Green Cabomba
- **Substrate:** Plain washed gravel
- **Lighting:** Bright
- **pH value:** Not critical
- **Hardness:** Not critical
- **Temperature:** 13-25°C (55-77°C)

Height: Unless regularly pruned, the stems of this vigorous aquatic plant can reach a length of 2m (6.5ft).
Distribution: Northern South America to southern North America.
Characteristics: The handsome submerged foliage consists of pale to dark green finely divided leaves, carried in opposite pairs on long thin stems. Linear floating leaves are produced when the yellow-centred white flowers are formed.
Aquarium use: An excellent bunch plant for the background.
Propagation: From terminal cuttings up to 30cm (12in) long. Remove the lower two or three pairs of leaves and plant in bunches of five or six stems.
Other species: *Cabomba aquatica*, with larger whorls of leaves and yellow flowers. *Cabomba piauhyensis*, in which the leaves and stems are reddish brown and the flowers yellow and purple.

Cardamine lyrata

Japanese Cress
- **Substrate:** Plain washed gravel
- **Lighting:** Bright
- **pH value:** Not critical
- **Hardness:** Not critical
- **Temperature:** 15-20°C (59-68°F)

Height: Up to 38cm (15in).
Distribution: Eastern China, Korea and Japan.
Characteristics: A pretty little moisture-loving plant that thrives when submerged in either coldwater or tropical aquariums. The delicate pale green leaves vary in shape according to growing conditions from almost circular to kidney-shaped with crenate margins. Aerial leaves are pinnate with large terminal lobes. Flowers are small and white.
Aquarium use: Background plant. Its delicate foliage makes a wonderful foil when planted with large clumps of *Cryptocoryne*. It will tolerate much higher temperatures than those recommended but will ultimately suffer and begin to wilt.
Propagation: By cuttings.

Below: **Cardamine lyrata**
A dependable background plant for brightly lit aquariums, ideally on the cooler side. Easy to propagate.

Above:
Ceratophyllum submersum
The delicate foliage of this floating plant can provide useful shade.

Ceratophyllum submersum

Tropical Hornwort
- **Substrate:** Not applicable
- **Lighting:** Bright
- **pH value:** Not critical
- **Hardness:** Not critical
- **Temperature:** 10-28°C (50-82°F)

Height: The plant tends to grow horizontally, reaching a length of 45cm (18in).
Distribution: Cosmopolitan.
Characteristics: An attractive aquatic plant with thin much-branched stems bearing whorls of bristle-like foliage. It is very brittle, breaking up easily even under the influence of gentle currents. The genera have lost the capacity to produce roots, even if treated with a rooting hormone preparation.
Aquarium use: An ideal floating plant that will act as a refuge for fry and discourage algae by filtering the light. Undemanding; clear warm water and abundant light are all it needs to thrive in the aquarium.
Propagation: Any piece that becomes detached from the mother plant will develop into a new plant.

Above and left:
Ceratopteris thalictroides
Two views of a variable plant that can grow completely submerged, on the surface or out of the water. A very versatile subject for aquarium use.

Ceratopteris thalictroides
Indian Fern
- **Substrate:** Peaty medium helps
- **Lighting:** Bright
- **pH value:** 5-6.5
- **Hardness:** 5-6°dH
- **Temperature:** 20-25°C (68-77°F)

Height: 38cm (15in).
Distribution: Widely distributed in tropical regions.
Characteristics: *Ceratopteris* is a true water fern that grows emersed, submersed and as a floating plant. Each of these forms has distinct differences in foliage. Emersed, the plant forms a rosette of much-branched cylindrical fronds or they may be broader and multipinnate. Submerged, the leaves are softer, broader and paler in colour. The floating form closely resembles the submerged one but the plant is flattened horizontally with white roots hanging free in the water. The normal colour is emerald green to dark green, but can be much paler depending on the light intensity and available nutrients in the aquarium.

Aquarium use: Variable according to the plant's form and habit. Large plants are ideal as middleground specimen plants. This fern will tolerate a wide range of water conditions, but is probably at its best in soft acid water, as indicated. Peaty medium used under the roots will help the plant to flourish. It demands good light; if grown under natural daylight in temperate regions it will die back during the winter months.
Propagation: This plant produces adventitious buds on older leaves. When these have developed into daughter plants about 4cm (1.6in) across, detach them and replant them in the substrate. Alternatively, allow these young plants to float on the surface, where they will reproduce themselves in the same manner and soon form a floating cover in the aquarium.

73

Crinum thaianum
Onion Plant
- **Substrate:** Plain washed gravel
- **Lighting:** Not critical
- **pH value:** Not critical
- **Hardness:** Not critical
- **Temperature:** 18-27°C (64-81°F)

Height: About 1.5 to 2m (5-6.5ft).
Distribution: Indo-Malayan region, especially Thailand.
Characteristics: An extremely attractive plant that grows from a large bulb, producing smooth straplike leaves 2.5-5cm (1-2in) wide in well-grown specimens. Leaf colour varies from light to dark green. The white lily-like flowers are generally only produced when the plant grows emersed. Viable seed is possible.
Aquarium use: A background plant for very deep aquariums.
Propagation: Offsets sometimes form on the bulbs and may be detached and replanted.
Other species: *C.natans* from Africa, another giant plant. The leaves have a puckered surface and undulating margins. *C.aquatica* from West Africa, a new introduction with thin, puckered, twisted leaves. This is a much smaller plant (up to 45cm/ 18in) and young plants are ideal for more modest aquariums. It is destined to become the most popular species once supplies are plentiful.

Cryptocoryne affinis
- **Substrate:** Plain washed gravel
- **Lighting:** Moderate
- **pH value:** 6.8-7.0
- **Hardness:** Not critical
- **Temperature:** 22-26°C (72-79°F)

Height: 15-30cm (6-12in).
Distribution: Southwestern Malayan Peninsula.
Characteristics: The leaves are soft, long and lanceolate, with short petioles. On freshly imported plants the leaves have a highly puckered surface and are normally a rather dirty brown. Under aquarium conditions, however, the leaves take on a beautiful emerald green hue, with the undersides bright red.
Aquarium use: Middleground. This is probably the hardiest of the Cryptocorynes. It will tolerate temperatures as low as 13°C (55°F) for a time but thrives in the recommended range. Water should be mildly acid to neutral, as indicated, and it will even grow in quite hard

Below: **Crinum thaianum**
Where space allows, this plant will provide a bold background to the aquarium. A very adaptable species.

Below right: **Cryptocoryne affinis**
An excellent subject for the middle of the aquarium. Undisturbed, it will propagate readily and spread out.

water, although it will be somewhat stunted in these conditions.
Propagation: Adult plants produce numerous runners and it will soon cover a wide area if left unchecked. Simply separate the daughter plants when they have established roots.

Cryptocoryne balansae

● **Substrate:** Plain washed gravel
● **Lighting:** Bright
● **pH value:** 7-7.5
● **Hardness:** Not critical
● **Temperature:** 22-27°C (72-81°F)

Height: 44-55cm (17-22in).
Distribution: Thailand, North Vietnam to China.
Characteristics: In the aquarium, the leaves are bright green and covered with indentations. They are carried on very short petioles only 4-5cm (1.5-2in) long. Imported plants are often reddish to brown.
Aquarium use: Background. Tanks need to be at least 45cm (18in) deep to accommodate this plant.
Propagation: Once established, the plant produces numerous runners.
Other species: C.usteriana is a very similar species from the Philippines, but much larger in all respects.

Above: **Cryptocoryne balansae**
Elegant and reasonably adaptable to aquarium conditions, this large plant will set off others to perfection.

Above: **Cryptocoryne blassii**
The olive-green leaves of this particular specimen act as a foil for the brighter greens of other plants in the tank. Use it in the background or as a solitary centrepiece plant.

Cryptocoryne blassii
Giant Cryp'
- **Substrate:** Plain washed gravel
- **Lighting:** Not critical
- **pH value:** Not critical
- **Hardness:** 5-11°dH
- **Temperature:** 25°C (77°F)

Height: 30-40cm (12-16in).
Distribution: Thailand.
Characteristics: A very striking plant bearing narrow ovate leaves with acute bases and bluntly pointed tips. The leaf surface may be quite puckered or it may be smooth. The colour of the upper surface varies from olive-green to wine-red; the underside is red. The leaves, up to 15cm (6in) long and 6.4cm (2.5in) wide, are borne on petioles about 10-15cm (4-6in) long.
Aquarium use: A background plant suitable for large aquariums not less than 50cm (20in) deep. Usually found growing on limestone, this species tolerates hard water well.
Propagation: Once established, it will send out a good number of runners. Do not separate these from the parent plant until they are well developed and have strong roots.

Cryptocoryne ciliata
- **Substrate:** Add iron-rich clay
- **Lighting:** Bright
- **pH value:** Not critical
- **Hardness:** Not critical
- **Temperature:** 20°C (68°F) minimum

Height: Although taller in the wild, aquarium specimens seldom exceed 50cm (20in).
Distribution: Widespread from the eastern states of India across the coastal areas of the Bay of Bengal to Thailand, the Malaysian Peninsula and then south east across the Indonesian islands to New Guinea.
Characteristics: Because of its vast natural range, this plant has produced several distinct varieties in which both the length and width of the leaves can vary. Basically, the leaves are lanceolate to broad lanceolate in shape and from pale to mid green in colour. The edges may be slightly wavy.
Aquarium use: Middleground to background, depending on the height of the aquarium. An easy species, very prolific once established. It will flourish even in

Above: **Cryptocoryne ciliata**
An easy, slow-growing plant that will adapt to different water conditions. Bright light and warmth are essential.

Above: **Cryptocoryne griffithii**
This is the typical spathe flower of the Cryptocorynes. It may be the only way of distinguishing certain species.

hard, slightly brackish water.
Propagation: By rhizome runners that produce young plants at intervals of about 10cm (4in). The plant is much easier and quicker to propagate when grown emersed.

Cryptocoryne griffithii
● **Substrate:** Add iron-rich clay
● **Lighting:** Moderate
● **pH value:** 6.5-7.0
● **Hardness:** 3-4°dH
● **Temperature:** 24-27°C (75-81°F)

Height: 25cm (10in) minimum.
Distribution: Malaysian Peninsula.
Characteristics: A very variable plant and much confused with *C. cordata* and *C. purpurea*. (Botanists disagree on the classification of these related species.) The broad ovate leaves with bluntly pointed tips reach a length of 7.5cm (3in) and a width of 5cm (2in). They are borne on petioles at least 20cm (8in) long. Their colour varies from pale to dark green or even dark brown on the upperside, and pale to dark green or often reddish on the underside. The upper surface is often streaked and blotched with brownish red markings.

Aquarium use: Middleground. A difficult plant to grow successfully, requiring soft, neutral to slightly acid water. It dislikes peat; a clay soil is necessary for luxuriant growth. Although in nature it is normally found in shady places and often covered in a deposit of iron-rich clay, in the aquarium it appreciates clean conditions with moderate lighting. It is very prone to 'Cryptocoryne rot' when first imported. (This condition causes plants to rot down to the base, but they then regrow. It can strike newly planted tanks and well-established aquariums alike. The exact cause and cure are unknown.) Remove all ragged and decaying leaves and float the plants in the tank for a week or so before planting.
Propagation: Slowly, by runners.

Cryptocoryne nevillii

Dwarf Cryp'

- **Substrate:** Fine gravel
- **Lighting:** Bright
- **pH value:** Not critical
- **Hardness:** Not critical
- **Temperature:** 20°C (68°F)
  minimum

Height: Variable. There appear to be two forms, one that reaches 6.4cm (2.5in) and one that grows up to 10cm (4in) in height.

Distribution: Sri Lanka.

Characteristics: The leaves, bright green on both upper and lower surfaces, are narrowly elliptical to lanceolate in shape and 5-10cm (2-4in) long, of which about two thirds is taken up by petioles.

Aquarium use: Foreground. Although slow to establish, it eventually forms nice rounded clumps. An easy species that needs bright light and clean water, but is otherwise undemanding. Use a finer grade of gravel than usual and leave it undisturbed as much as possible.

Propagation: By short runners. Once separated, float the daughter plants in the tank for a few weeks; the numerous side shoots that develop provide a way of increasing the numbers quite quickly.

Cryptocoryne retrospiralis

- **Substrate:** Plain washed gravel
- **Lighting:** Bright
- **pH value:** 7-7.2
- **Hardness:** 14-15°dH
- **Temperature:** 20°C (68°F)
  minimum

Above: **Cryptocoryne retrospiralis**
Position this plant in the middle, sides or back of the aquarium. Very easy to propagate from runners.

Left: **Cryptocoryne nevillii**
A superb easy-care plant for the foreground. Once established, it will put on healthy looking growth.

Height: Up to 30cm (12in).
Distribution: India to Thailand and Laos.
Characteristics: Leaves are linear to straplike with sharply pointed tips and acute bases. The leaf blades, slightly puckered and with wavy margins, range in colour from pale green through dark green to brown, depending on the locality from which the plants have been collected.
Aquarium use: A middleground to background plant, depending on aquarium depth.
Propagation: Once established, it produces runners readily.

Cryptocoryne wendtii

- **Substrate:** Plain washed gravel
- **Lighting:** Moderate to bright
- **pH value:** 6.8-7.2
- **Hardness:** 3-8°dH
- **Temperature:** 20-26°C (68-79°F)

Height: Dwarf varieties up to 13cm (5in); larger ones up to 20cm (8in).

Distribution: Sri Lanka.
Characteristics: An extremely
variable species depending on the
area from which it is collected. The
type plant *C.wendtii* var. *wendtii* has
egg-shaped to ovate leaves with a
prominent midrib and wavy margins.
The upper surface is pale to olive-
green, with faint dark green striations;
the underside is pale green to light
brown in colour.
Aquarium use: Foreground to
middleground, according to variety.
A very adaptable species.
Propagation: By runners.
Other varieties: *C.wendtii* var.
jahnelii, the largest form. *C.wendtii*
var. *krauteri*, similar to the type
species but with a more definitely
flecked upper leaf surface. *C.wendtii*
var. *nana*, the dwarf form. *C.wendtii*

var. *rubella*, with reddish leaves. Over
60 species of Cryptocorynes are
currently recognized and more are
undoubtedly waiting to be
discovered. Thus we have featured
only a few 'typical' species in this
book. However, the Cryptocorynes
fall into three distinct groups and in
general terms plants from the same
group require similar treatment.

Group One: The *C.wendtii* Group
Includes *C.beckettii*, *C.legroi*,
C.lucens, *C.lutea*, *C.parva*, *C.petchii*,
C.thwaitesii, *C.walkeri*, *C.willisii*.

Below: **Cryptocoryne wendtii**
*A very variable species that can be
used at the front or in the middle of the
aquarium. There are many varieties to
choose from. Easy to propagate.*

Group Two: The *C.griffithii* Group
Includes *C.auriculata*, *C.cordata*,
C.johorensis, *C.minima*, *C.nurri*,
C.siamensis, *C.purpurea*, *C.shultzei*.

Group Three: The *Cryptocoryne
retrospiralis* Group
Includes *C.albida*, *C.costata*,
C.spiralis

Didiplis diandra
Water Hedge
- **Substrate:** Plain washed gravel
- **Lighting:** Subdued
- **pH value:** Not critical
- **Hardness:** Not critical
- **Temperature:** 18°C (64°F)

Height: 30cm (12in).
Distribution: On wet habitats in
southern North America.

Characteristics: A pretty little plant
with pale green linear leaves borne on
a thin, much-branched stem. The
leaves are about 2.5cm (1in) long and
3mm (0.12in) wide. Because of its
unusual form, this plant makes an
ideal contrast to the heavier leaves of
the Cryptocorynes, and is often used
in fully planted aquariums.

Aquarium use: Middleground plant.
It can tolerate a wide range of water
conditions and flourishes in crowded
tanks under light shade.

Propagation: Take stem cuttings
about 10cm (4in) long.

Below: **Didiplis diandra**
*The graceful stems and leaves of this
undemanding North American plant
can be used to lighten the effect of
any heavier plants in the aquarium.*

Echinodorus cordifolius
Radicans Sword; Spade-leaf Plant
- **Substrate:** Rich
- **Lighting:** Bright
- **pH value:** Not critical
- **Hardness:** Not critical
- **Temperature:** 10-27°C (50-81°F)

Height: Up to 60cm (24in).
Distribution: Southern North America.
Characteristics: Broad egg-shaped leaves up to 23cm (9in) long and 18cm (7in) wide are produced when the plant is grown submerged, varying considerably in length between different individuals. The leaves are light green but under certain conditions small purple blotches may appear.
Aquarium use: Specimen plant. Very hardy in the aquarium, it tolerates both soft and hard water but likes a rich substrate. However, if

Above: **Echinodorus cordifolius**
This outstanding species is very well established in aquarium circles, long cultivated for its form and resilience.

exposed to more than 12 hours of light per day it has a tendency to throw up aerial leaves. Plants received from suppliers will always be grown emersed. Although the older leaves die off when the plant is submerged, new underwater leaves will soon take their place. Prune the roots of emersed grown plants severely before submersion.
Propagation: Easily propagated in an emersed state; mature plants produce two or three aerial shoots that bear flowers and then seeds or adventitious plantlets. Sow the seeds in shallow pans as soon as they are ripe. Peg down the plantlets into mini-pots and separate them from the parent plant when 10cm (4in) high.

Echinodorus major
Ruffled Amazon Sword
- **Substrate:** Rich
- **Lighting:** Bright
- **pH value:** Not critical
- **Hardness:** 3-18°dH
- **Temperature:** 20-25°C (68-77°F)

Height: Up to 50cm (20in), normally considerably smaller.
Distribution: Brazil.
Characteristics: The long straplike leaves are pale green in colour, somewhat transluscent in appearance, with a distinctive pattern of veins. The edges are highly undulated, which accounts for the plant's common name. Petioles are very short.
Aquarium use: A specimen plant for large aquariums.
Propagation: Submersed, the plant throws up a stem on which adventitious plantlets develop. Emersed, these stems produce flowers and seed. The seed is very small and germinates quickly, but it will take two years to produce plants of useable size. The adventitious plantlets are ideal for propagation.

Below: **Echinodorus major**
Ensure that this vigorous plant has sufficient nutrients to develop fully in the aquarium. Given space, it can develop into an eye-catching subject. Grow it in bright unobstructed light.

Echinodorus paniculatus

(Also known as E.bleheri)
Broad-leaf Amazon Sword
- **Substrate:** Rich, with clay
- **Lighting:** Not critical
- **pH value:** Not critical
- **Hardness:** Not critical
- **Temperature:** 20-27°C (68-81°F)

Height: Up to 38cm (15in).
Distribution: Widely distributed in South America.
Characteristics: The lanceolate leaves are pale to dark green with sharply pointed tips. The petiole is short in aquarium-grown plants but very long in imported specimens due to the commercial practice of growing them very close together, forcing the petioles to lengthen as the leaves reach for the light.
Aquarium use: An excellent specimen plant for the middleground. This is the most popular Amazon Swordplant because of its hardiness and tolerance of hard/alkaline water

Above: **Echinodorus paniculatus**
The broad leaves of this Amazon Swordplant stand out well amid other aquarium subjects. Very dependable.

Below: **Echinodorus tenellus**
This robust foreground plant will quickly form a dense carpet of foliage over the aquarium substrate.

Above: **Egeria densa**
A well-known aquarium plant prized for its attractive growth and valued as an adaptable background plant.

conditions. It thrives with clay in the substrate, ideally with abundant trace elements added at regular intervals.
Propagation: The aerial stems seldom flower but bear numerous plantlets. Peg these stems down on to the aquarium substrate and separate them from the mother plant when they are about 15cm (6in) high. It is also possible to divide old plants.
Other varieties: Several varieties are available, including a narrow-leafed form offered commercially as the Narrow Leaf Amazon.

Echinodorus tenellus
Pygmy Chain Swordplant
● **Substrate:** Plain washed gravel
● **Lighting:** Not critical
● **pH value:** 6.5-7.2
● **Hardness:** 3-18°dH
● **Temperature:** 15-26 (59-79°F)

Height: There are several races and growing forms of this plant. The standard variety reaches a height of 15cm (6in), but both smaller and larger specimens exist.
Distribution: North America, from Michigan to Florida. South America, from Colombia to southern Brazil.
Characteristics: Emerse, the plant produces petioles about 7.5cm (3in) long, each topped with a lanceolate leaf about 2.5cm (1in) long and acute at both ends. Such emerse-grown plants produce an inflorescence of numerous small white flowers. When grown submerged, the plants lose the petioles and produce lanceolate leaves up to 15cm (6in) in length. In crowded conditions these stand upright, but where room allows they will curve over and reduce the height of the plant to 5cm (2in). Of the numerous subspecies, some from northern ranges will stand lower temperatures than the type. Others are larger or smaller than the type. However, the standard type described above seems to pervade the commercial market because many of the other varieties come from seldom collected areas.
Aquarium use: As a foreground groundcover plant or even as a specimen plant in small tanks. An accommodating species.
Propagation: Normally by runners, which are very prolific and ideal for propagation. Also by seed, freely produced in emerse-grown plants.

Egeria densa
Giant Elodea
● **Substrate:** Plain washed gravel
● **Lighting:** Bright
● **pH value:** 7-8
● **Hardness:** 20-25°dH
● **Temperature:** 10-25°C (50-77°F)

Height: Up to 1.8m (6ft) in length.
Distribution: South and Central America.
Characteristics: The green stems are sparsely branched with three or four narrowly lanceolate green leaves arranged in whorls.
Aquarium use: A background plant for both temperate and tropical aquariums. In soft neutral water the plant is thinner and paler in colour than in the recommended conditions.
Propagation: By cuttings. Also, new shoots from the creeping rootstock.

Eleocharis acicularis
Dwarf Hairgrass
- **Substrate:** Some clay of benefit
- **Lighting:** Bright
- **pH value:** Not critical
- **Hardness:** Not critical
- **Temperature:** 10-25°C (50-77°F)

Height: Up to 20cm (8in), but usually smaller in aquarium specimens.
Distribution: Worldwide in all the warmer regions.
Characteristics: Grasslike plant growing in rosettes. The leaves are hairlike and are rich green in well-nourished plants.
Aquarium use: A carpet-forming plant suitable for foreground planting in both heated and unheated aquariums. Produces numerous runners and soon forms a thick turf. Some clay incorporated into the substrate will encourage sturdy growth in the aquarium.
Propagation: By runners.
Other species: *Eleocharis vivipara*, the Umbrella Hairgrass and *E.xingua*, a much larger species.

Below: **Eleocharis acicularis**
The combination of rich green and grasslike form makes this a useful

Gymnocoronis spilanthoides
Spade-leaf Plant
- **Substrate:** Rich
- **Lighting:** Bright
- **pH value:** Not critical
- **Hardness:** Not critical
- **Temperature:** 20-25°C (68-77°F)

Height: 30-40cm (12-16in).
Distribution: Tropical regions of South America.
Characteristics: A thick fleshy herbaceous perennial with stout stems up to 15mm (0.6in) thick. The large bright green leaves are elliptical to lanceolate in shape and reach a length of 12.5cm (5in) and a width of 3.8cm (1.5in). They have subtle undulating margins.
Aquarium use: A background plant. It grows rapidly and will need frequent pruning, after which it will produce abundant side shoots. An excellent plant for filling space quickly in a tropical aquarium. It is indifferent to the pH value and water hardness.
Propagation: Cuttings.

subject for creating attractive plantings in the aquarium. Suitable for both temperate and tropical tanks.

Above: **Heteranthera zosterifolia**
The distinctive shape of this South American species adds visual interest in the centre of this mixed planting. A hardy subject for the aquarium.

Heteranthera zosterifolia
Water Stargrass
● **Substrate:** Rich, with clay
● **Lighting:** Bright
● **pH value:** 7-8
● **Hardness:** Not critical
● **Temperature:** 18-27°C (64-81°C)

Height: 1m (39in).
Distribution: Brazil, Bolivia and adjacent parts of South America.
Characteristics: A perennial water plant that grows submerged for long periods. The leaves are two-ranked, ribbon-shaped and bright green, about 5cm (2in) long and 3-7mm (0.12-0.28in) wide.
Aquarium use: Middle to background. An undemanding and hardy species, ideally planted in bunches of four or five stems.
Propagation: Cuttings. Use top pieces 10-15cm (4-6in) long and plant them in bunches.

Above:
Gymnocoronis spilanthoides
In a rich substrate, this plant rapidly forms a dense background.

Hottonia inflata

Tropical Water Violet
- **Substrate:** Rich
- **Lighting:** Bright
- **pH value:** Not critical
- **Hardness:** Not critical
- **Temperature:** 18-23°C (64-73°F)

Height: Up to 60cm (24in).
Distribution: Southeastern North America.
Characteristics: Multibranched stems bear alternate pinnate leaves of bright green. Although only recently introduced into cultivation, this plant is now readily available.
Aquarium use: A background bunch plant. A hardy species that thrives in clear, clean water and a rich substrate.
Propagation: By cuttings 15cm (6in) long. Prepare these in the usual way.

Below: **Hottonia inflata**
A relative newcomer to the aquarium hobby, this plant thrives in a rich substrate and bright lighting.

Above: **Hydrocotyle vulgaris**
An excellent choice for an appealing green fringe in the foreground.

Hydrocotyle vulgaris

Pennywort; Umbrella plant
- **Substrate:** Fine gravel
- **Lighting:** Bright
- **pH value:** Not critical
- **Hardness:** Not critical
- **Temperature:** 10-25°C (50-77°F)

Height: 5-7.5cm (2-3in).
Distribution: Europe.
Characteristics: A delightful little

plant with circular mid green leaves borne atop slender stems. The leaves reach 2.5cm (1in) in diameter.

Aquarium use: A foreground plant. Undemanding with regard to water conditions, this plant thrives in both cool and tropical conditions. It benefits from a finer grade of gravel than the other species of the genus. It will flourish in a well-lit aquarium but may die back for a short period during the winter months.

Propagation: By runners.

Other species: H.leucocephala from South America and H.verticillata from southeastern North America and Central America. Both species make good subjects for tropical aquariums but are unsuitable for the foreground; plant them further back for the best effect. Both have a tendency to produce floating leaves.

Below: **Hygrophila polysperma**
A popular aquarium plant that will establish quickly and grow strongly in a wide range of water conditions.

Hygrophila polysperma
Dwarf Hygrophila

- **Substrate:** Plain washed gravel
- **Lighting:** Bright
- **pH value:** Not critical
- **Hardness:** Not critical
- **Temperature:** 15-30°C (59-86°F)

Height: Up to 45cm (18in).
Distribution: Southeast Asia.
Characteristics: A small-leaved herbaceous plant that grows well both emersed and submersed. The leaves, broadly lanceolate with rounded tips and up to 5cm (2in) by 15mm (0.6in), are borne in opposite pairs on thin stems. The colour is pale to mid green, with reddish tips developing in bright light.
Aquarium use: An undemanding bunch plant for the background. It looks especially striking when planted against a dark backdrop in the aquarium. Be sure to clear all snails from the aquarium: they seem to relish all species of *Hygrophila*!
Propagation: By cuttings.

Hygrophila salicifolia
(Also known as H.angustifolia)
Willow-leaf Hygrophila
- **Substrate:** Plain washed gravel
- **Lighting:** Bright
- **pH value:** Not critical
- **Hardness:** Not critical
- **Temperature:** 21-26°C (70-79°F)

Height: 38cm (15in).
Distribution: Southeast Asia.
Characteristics: A more robust species than *H.polysperma*, with reddish stems that grow bolt upright. The leaves are opposite, slender lanceolate and dark green in colour. They closely resemble those of the willow, from which the plant derives its common name. Small white flowers are borne in dense clusters in the axils of the leaves.
Aquarium use: Middle to background plant, depending on the height of the aquarium. An easy and effective subject requiring good light and clear water.
Propagation: By cuttings.
Other species: There are many species of *Hygrophila* and new ones are being discovered all the time. Those in regular supply include: *H.lacustris* from Thailand, with pale green lanceolate leaves up to 10cm (4in) long; *H.difformis* from mainland Southeast Asia, a beautiful plant with variable entire or pinnate leaves; *H.siamensis* and *H.costata*. No doubt some of these names will be changed by earnest taxonomists.

Lagenandra thwaitesii
- **Substrate:** Rich
- **Lighting:** Very bright
- **pH value:** Not critical
- **Hardness:** Not critical
- **Temperature:** 25°C (77°F)

Height: Up to 45cm (18in).
Distribution: Sri Lanka.
Characteristics: A perennial bog plant with dark green lanceolate leaves edged in greyish silver. The leaves reach a length of 23cm (9in) and a width of 3.8cm (1.5in) with a petiole of 23cm (9in).
Aquarium use: Either as a specimen plant for the middleground or in batches of two or three as a background feature. Give Lagenandras strong light and a rich bottom soil, regularly fertilized.
Propagation: The tuberous rootstock produces smaller plants along its length. Divide the rootstock with a sharp knife, ensuring that each piece has a growing shoot.

Below: **Lagenandra thwaitesii**
A dense growth of this perennial species photographed in its natural bog habitat in Sri Lanka.

Above: **Hygrophila salicifolia**
A dependable medium-sized subject suitable for either the middleground or background of a tropical aquarium.

Below: **Lagenandra thwaitesii**
A single leaf of this plant showing the attractive greyish silver edging.

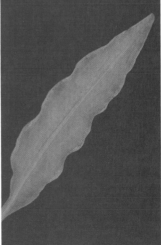

Lilaeopsis novae-zelandiae

- **Substrate:** Rich, with clay
- **Lighting:** Bright
- **pH value:** Not critical
- **Hardness:** Not critical
- **Temperature:** 18-25°C (64-77°F)

Height: Up to 8cm (3.2in), but normally only half this.

Distribution: New Zealand.

Characteristics: Each plant consists of one to three mid green ribbon-like leaves, often with flattened tips. There is no petiole. It has not flowered so far under aquarium conditions.

Aquarium use: A carpet-forming species that forms an excellent foreground subject for both cool and tropical aquariums. This delightful newcomer thrives in crystal-clear water and a rich substrate composed of 3mm (0.125in) gravel overlaying an iron-rich clay soil.

Propagation: A very prolific plant. *Lilaeopsis* will cover the substrate at an incredible rate, each plant producing several runners that bear independent daughter plants.

Above: **Limnobium laevigatum**
This top view emphasizes how the rosettes of this tropical plant lie flat on the surface of the water.

Below:
Lilaeopsis novae-zelandiae
A vigorous foreground subject. Give bright light and a rich substrate.

Above: **Limnophila aquatica**
An ideal plant to disguise those necessary but unattractive pieces of aquarium equipment. It grows quite large, so trim it to keep it in check.

Limnobium laevigatum

The Amazon Frogbit
- **Substrate:** Not applicable
- **Lighting:** Bright
- **pH value:** Not critical
- **Hardness:** Not critical
- **Temperature:** 20-30°C (68-86°F)

Height: The leaves lie flat on the surface of the water.
Distribution: Mexico to Paraguay.
Characteristics: A rosette-forming plant. The leaves, round with a cordate base, have short petioles and contain spongy tissue that makes them buoyant and slightly convex in shape. They are 2.5-5cm (1-2in) in diameter, olive-green – often with striated markings – above, pale green below. The white roots may reach a length of 30cm (12in). Male and female flowers are produced on separate plants; so far only female plants are available commercially.
Aquarium use: A floating plant with long trailing roots that shade the aquarium and act as an excellent spawning site and fry refuge for many fishes. As with all floating plants, be sure to fit a cover glass on the aquarium to stop them burning up under the lights, and also to maintain the humidity at saturation point. To encourage good growth, provide bright light and nutrient-rich water. Dose the aquarium regularly with trace elements and a general purpose liquid fertilizer.
Propagation: By division of the numerous runners.

Limnophila aquatica

Giant Ambulia
- **Substrate:** Plain washed gravel
- **Lighting:** Bright
- **pH value:** 6-7
- **Hardness:** Not critical
- **Temperature:** 20-25°C (68-77°F)

Height: Up to 50cm (20in).
Distribution: India and Sri Lanka.
Characteristics: The thick stems support very fine pinnate or bipinnate leaves arranged in whorls of 3-10. The plant has a tendency to run to the surface, where it produces dark green aerial leaves of a simple lanceolate shape with toothed margins. Flowers are pale blue with darker streaks.
Aquarium use: Use this plant in small bunches of three or four stems to hide filters and heaters at the back of the tank. Prune it regularly to retain its attractive shape. Although generally easy to grow in the aquarium, Giant Ambulia does need good light to thrive; plants taken from poorly lit sources do not recover their vigour. And be sure to keep the water well filtered; in common with other fine-leaved plants, it will suffer if general aquarium detritus becomes trapped in the foliage.
Propagation: Take cuttings 15cm (6in) long, including the growing tip. Strip the leaves from the lower 4cm (1.6in) of stem.
Other species: *Limnophila sessiflora* (Dwarf Ambulia), a much finer plant ideal for smaller aquariums.

Ludwigia mullertii
Red Ludwigia

- **Substrate:** Plain washed gravel
- **Lighting:** Bright
- **pH value:** Not critical
- **Hardness:** Not critical
- **Temperature:** 14-26°C (57-79°F)

Height: Up to 38cm (15in).

Distribution: This plant is reputed to be a hybrid of *Ludwigia repens* and *L.palustris*, both of which occur in some areas of North America.

Characteristics: A herbaceous plant with long multibranched stems bearing elliptical leaves up to 3cm (1.2in) long and 15mm (0.5in) wide on short petioles.

Aquarium use: A free-growing bunch plant suitable for the middleground or background,

Below: **Ludwigia mullertii**
This strongly growing plant will provide a bold accent to brighten up the background of a mixed planting.

Above: **Marsilea crenata**
As a contrast to more conspicuous plants, this delightful species brings a delicate touch to the foreground.

depending on the height of the aquarium. Its red leaves provide a useful foil for predominantly green plants. Prune it regularly to keep it from becoming straggly and provide abundant light; in poor light it will lose its red coloration.
Propagation: By cuttings. It will also produce viable seed from tiny flowers when grown emersed.

Marsilea crenata
Dwarf Four-leaf Clover
● **Substrate:** Fine gravel
● **Lighting:** Not critical
● **pH value:** Not critical
● **Hardness:** Not critical
● **Temperature:** 18°C (64°C) minimum

Height: Up to 8cm (3.2in).
Distribution: Southeast Asia.
Characteristics: A tiny creeping plant with thin upright stems each of

which bears a four-part frond (sometimes only two-part) with blades up to 1cm (0.4in) long and 5mm (0.2in) wide. It remains permanently submerged and produces no floating leaves. Despite appearances, the genus is closely allied to the ferns.
Aquarium use: Foreground carpeting plant. Easy to grow in the aquarium, although it benefits from a finer grained substrate than usual.
Propagation: By runners, freely produced by established plants.
Other species: *M.quadrifolia*, now less commonly available, is a much larger, almost hardy plant that invariably runs to the top and produces floating leaves.

requirements, but is best grown in subdued light; in bright light transparent patches form on the fronds. Do not plant it in the gravel; simply attach it to bogwood or rockwork using rubber bands.
Propagation: By division of adult specimens or from the adventitious plantlets that form on older leaves. Attach the plantlets to pieces of bogwood and they will soon take hold with their roots.

Left: **Myriophyllum hippuroides**
This is one of many species from the Water Milfoil Family that grace tropical and temperate aquariums the world over. In bright light and clean water, it is a very adaptable plant.

Right: **Microsorium pteropus**
An interesting aquarium plant that thrives at low light levels and attaches itself to rocks and bogwood.

Microsorium pteropus
Java Fern
- **Substrate:** Not applicable
- **Lighting:** Subdued
- **pH value:** Not critical
- **Hardness:** Not critical
- **Temperature:** 20-25°C (68-77°F)

Height: 25cm (10in).
Distribution: Widely distributed in tropical Southeast Asia.
Characteristics: Java Fern grows from a thick rhizome that creeps over logs and rockwork, attaching itself by its roots as it goes. Short-stalked, lanceolate fronds up to 25cm (10in) long and 3cm (1.2in) wide are produced underwater. These fronds are leathery in texture and mid to dark green in colour. Aerial fronds are often divided into tripartitie blades at the top. (Another fern species with much thinner rhizomes and stems is often sold commercially as Java Fern. It is collected in Malaya and does not thrive underwater.)
Aquarium use: As a decorative plant for clothing bogwood and rocks. An easy going plant that in the wild grows attached to tree trunks and rocks in the jungle. Although it normally grows emersed, it does equally well underwater. It is hardy and undemanding, with no special water

Myriophyllum hippuroides

- **Substrate:** Plain washed gravel
- **Lighting:** Bright
- **pH value:** Not critical
- **Hardness:** Not critical
- **Temperature:** 15-25°C (59-77°F)

Height: Up to 45cm (18in).

Distribution: North and Central America.

Characteristics: An aquatic plant with long thin stems supporting 5cm (2in) leaves in whorls of four to six. Colour is olive-green to reddish, depending on the level of illumination.

Aquarium use: Background bunch plant. In common with other Milfoils, this species demands clean, clear water with no trace of floating detritus to clog the delicate leaves. Prune all Milfoils regularly to prevent them becoming straggly and cut them back when they reach the surface.

Propagation: Take cuttings. Strip the lower three pairs of leaves before planting the cuttings in bunches of four to five stems.

Other species: M.brasiliense (Parrot's Feather), which grows best in an emersed state and is much used in outdoor water gardening. M.mattogrossense, which has bright red foliage. M.elatinoides, similar but coarser than M.hippuroides. Species such as Myriophyllum spicatum and M.verticillatum are only suitable for temperate aquariums.

Nomaphila stricta
Giant Hygrophila
- **Substrate:** Rich
- **Lighting:** Bright
- **pH value:** Not critical
- **Hardness:** Not critical
- **Temperature:** 20°C (68°F) minimum

Height: Up to 45cm (18in).
Distribution: Southeast Asia.
Characteristics: A large herbaceous plant that inhabits marshy areas. It has both emersed and submersed growth patterns. Underwater, the thick green stems bear opposite, broad lanceolate leaves with pointed tips and long petioles. They reach a length of 12cm (4.7in) and a width of 4cm (1.6in) and are bright green in colour. Specimens grown out of water become woody, with more rounded darker leaves that may be almost purple in colour. The flowers are bright blue and sweetly scented. There is much confusion between *Nomaphila* and *Hygrophila*. This species is called *Hygrophila corymbosa* by some authorities.

Aquarium use: Background plant. Group three or four stems in close proximity for the best effect. An undemanding plant that likes a rich substrate and good illumination. Ensure that the aquarium is completely free from snails; they appear to relish this species.
Propagation: Take cuttings 15cm (6in) in length.
Other species: Several other species from Southeast Asia are now often available commercially, but their true identification has yet to be decided by botanists.

Below: **Nomaphila stricta**
This distinctive plant stands out clearly among other aquarium plants.

Right: **Nuphar japonicum**
Where space permits, this splendid plant makes a bold impact in the tank.

Nuphar japonicum
Japanese Spatterdock
- **Substrate:** Rich, with clay
- **Lighting:** Bright
- **pH value:** Not critical
- **Hardness:** Not critical
- **Temperature:** 12-25°C (54-77°F)

Height: Up to 60cm (24in).

Distribution: Japan and adjacent islands. Now introduced into Java.

Characteristics: Fleshy petioles up to 30cm (12in) or more in length arise from a creeping white rootstock up to 3.8cm (1.5in) in diameter. The petioles bear roundly arrow-shaped, pale green leaves up to 30cm (12in) long and 12cm (4.7in) wide.

Aquarium use: As a specimen plant for larger aquariums. This close relative of the Water Lily Family needs similar conditions for successful growth. A little clay added to the bottom soil, plus some solid fertilizer, will work wonders. And pay particular attention to the rhizome when you receive it. Cut out any decayed portions, cauterize the cut and rub in a little powdered charcoal and sulphur to prevent further decay.

Propagation: By division of the rhizome. Make each cutting about 7.5cm (3in) long and ensure that it has a growing point and a good number of healthy roots.

Other species and varieties: Other species include *N.sagittifolium* from the southern United States, with fairly narrow leaves. *N.lutea* which, although a native of Eurasia, will succeed in tropical aquariums. *N.japonicum* var. *rubrotinctum* from the islands to the north of Japan has darker leaves than the type species.

Nymphaea maculata
African Tiger Lotus
- **Substrate:** Plain washed gravel
- **Lighting:** Bright
- **pH value:** Not critical
- **Hardness:** Not critical
- **Temperature:** 20-30°C (68-86°F)

Height: Up to 45cm (18in).
Distribution: West Africa.
Characteristics: This species has two forms, known commercially as the Red Tiger Lotus and the Green Tiger Lotus. The leaves in both types are rounded and wavy, with the typical deep indentation at the base. In the red variety, the upper leaf surface may be brownish to red with darker blotches. The underside is a vivid purple. The leaves of the green variety are mid green with purple blotches on the upper surface and pale green beneath. The leaves in both types, always submerged, reach

Above: **Nymphaea maculata**
These large leaves bring welcome new shapes to the aquarium.

a diameter of 15cm (6in). The white flowers, supported above the water surface, open at night and are up to 6cm (2.4in) in diameter.
Aquarium use: Normally used as a specimen plant. As a typical tropical water lily, the African Tiger Lotus starts life as a small rounded tuber up to 3.8cm (1.5in) in diameter. Simply plant this in the aquarium gravel and add a proprietary water lily fertilizing capsule. In the recommended temperature range and in bright light the plant will develop rapidly.
Propagation: Several shoots may arise from the tuber; simply separate one or more of these to gain extra plants. The plant will bloom in the aquarium and set seeds. These fall to the bottom and readily sprout.

Nymphaea stellata
Red and Blue Water Lilies
- **Substrate:** Plain washed gravel
- **Lighting:** Bright
- **pH value:** Not critical
- **Hardness:** Not critical
- **Temperature:** 20-28°C (68-82°F)

Height: Wild plants grow to enormous sizes, with leaves up to 30cm (12in) in diameter.

Distribution: Southern and eastern Asia and neighbouring islands.

Characteristics: The small rounded tubers, about 2.5cm (1in) in diameter, produce arrow-shaped brownish green leaves on petioles about 10cm (4in) long. They will soon start to throw leaves with longer petioles that grow towards the surface. The terms 'red' and 'blue' refer to the flower colour of the adult plants.

Aquarium use: As specimen plants. Although these water lilies are

Above: **Nymphaea stellata**
Keep these potentially large plants in check by pruning them regularly.

capable of reaching far larger proportions than can be accommodated in aquariums, it is possible to encourage the smaller juvenile growth to persist by rigorously pruning any stems that attempt to reach the surface. These tropical water lilies need bright light but are adaptable to most water conditions. Do not fertilize them; this will encourage them to bolt to the surface of the water.

Propagation: These plants are normally bought in fresh every year from Sri Lanka and propagation is not attempted.

Other species: The Thai Lotus, a similar plant with larger tubers, is often offered for sale. Treat as directed for *Nymphaea stellata*.

Nymphoides aquatica
Banana Plant
- **Substrate:** Plain washed gravel
- **Lighting:** Sunny
- **pH value:** Not critical
- **Hardness:** Not critical
- **Temperature:** 20-25°C (68-77°F)

Height: About 30cm (12in).
Distribution: Atlantic coast of the United States.
Characteristics: A perennial plant with a short stem. The swollen tubercles that form on the rootstock resemble a bunch of bananas (hence the common name) and act as storage organs to enable the plant to withstand drying out. Long petioles bear circular leaves that are bright green or reddish in colour and have a tendency to float. Small white flowers are carried above the surface on stalks growing in the axils of leaves.
Aquarium use: An aquarium oddity. Banana plants thrive in shallow water and warm sunny conditions.
Propagation: By dividing the rootstock, from runners or by detaching adventitious plantlets.

Pistia stratiotes
Water Lettuce
- **Substrate:** Not applicable
- **Lighting:** Bright
- **pH value:** 6.5-7.0
- **Hardness:** 3-6°dH
- **Temperature:** 22°C (72°F) minimum

Height: A large floating plant.
Distribution: Cosmopolitan in tropical and some subtropical areas.
Characteristics: A floating plant with leaves arranged in rosette formation. The leaves are light green and hairy, strap-shaped with blunt ends and up to 10cm (4in) long. The white trailing roots may reach 30cm (12in) in length.
Aquarium use: Useful for providing shade, spawning sites and as a refuge for fry. It is not the easiest plant to grow under artificial light but if successful, it will produce hundreds of tiny plants up to 2.5cm (1in) across. Any large plants will either burn up under the lights or succumb to various fungal and bacterial infections. Fit a cover glass but angle

Above: **Nymphoides aquatica**
A curiosity for the aquarium, with swollen roots that resemble a bunch of bananas. Provide warmth and sun.

it so that droplets of condensation do not fall on the plants and spoil them.
Propagation: By detaching daughter plants on runners, freely produced by well-established plants.

Riccia fluitans
Crystalwort
- **Substrate:** Plain washed gravel
- **Lighting:** Bright
- **pH value:** Ideally 6.8
- **Hardness:** Not critical
- **Temperature:** 20-26°C (68-79°F)

Height: A floating plant.
Distribution: Cosmopolitan in both tropical and temperate areas.
Characteristics: *Riccia* belongs to the Liverwort Family and is one of only two known aquatic species of liverworts. The plant body, or thallus, is made up of bright green ribbon-shaped growths that fork frequently to form thick balls that float just below the surface of the water. If grown

Above: **Pistia stratiotes**
A top view of this vigorous floating plant. Keep it in check before it casts too much shade in the aquarium.

Below: **Riccia fluitans**
A simple plant that builds into a bundle of green ribbons floating on and just below the water surface.

terrestrially, it forms root structures called rhizoids that anchor the thallus to the substrate. In this state, it produces spore capsules as the culmination of sexual reproduction. Aquatic forms reproduce asexually.

Aquarium use: To provide shade, fry refuges and spawning sites for Anabantids and other fishes.
Propagation: Any portion of the thallus that breaks away is capable of forming a new plant.

103

Rotala macrandra

Giant Red Rotala

- **Substrate:** Plain washed gravel
- **Lighting:** Very bright
- **pH value:** Not critical
- **Hardness:** Not critical
- **Temperature:** 25°C (77°F) minimum

Height: Up to 45cm (18in).
Distribution: India.
Characteristics: A herbaceous plant with elongated shoots that bear egg-shaped or elliptical leaves in opposite pairs. The upper side of the leaf blade is pale green; the underside bright pink or red. They are up to 3cm (1.2in) long and 15mm (0.6in) wide.
Aquarium use: An excellent plant for adding contrast to middleground and background plantings. The bright red lower leaf surfaces show up well against green plants nearby. This beautiful plant has proved difficult to cultivate under aquarium conditions, however. It is very soft and thus easily bruised in transit. It has not proved amenable to cultivation in temperate aquatic nurseries under natural daylight. Some hobbyists have managed to get reasonable results by giving it 12 hours of quartz halogen lighting per day.
Propagation: From cuttings.
Other species: The less well-known species *Rotala rotundifolia*, smaller in all respects than *R.macrandra*, is very

Below: **Rotala macrandra**
The rich colours of this light-loving species add welcome warmth to the cool greens that abound in aquariums.

Above: **Sagittaria platyphylla**
Use this species where it will show its bold form to advantage. Keep it brightly lit and well nourished.

easy to grow in the aquarium. Its submerged foliage is narrow but shows the same bright coloration of its larger relative. *R. wallichii*, another colourful and undemanding species, has almost filamentous leaves.

Sagittaria platyphylla
Giant Sagittaria
- **Substrate:** Rich
- **Lighting:** Very bright
- **pH value:** Not critical
- **Hardness:** Not critical
- **Temperature:** 15-25°C (59-77°F)

Height: Up to 40cm (16in).
Distribution: Southern North America, in the lower region of the Mississippi. Naturalized widely.
Characteristics: Submerged, the leaves are linear with pointed tips, mid green in colour and up to 40cm (16in) long and 2cm (0.8in) wide. This species has a tendency to grow out of the water, producing broad lanceolate or oval aerial leaves borne on petioles. In this state, the plant produces white flowers and subsequently seed capsules.
Aquarium use: As a background plant in quantity, or use two or three individuals to create a fine centrepiece. Be sure to provide a rich substrate for this gross feeder, and fertilize it regularly. It needs at least 12 hours of intense light a day to flourish.
Propagation: By runners. If allowed to hibernate outside, however, it will produce small tubers. Store these in cool water for a couple of months before planting them in the aquarium.

Above:
Sagittaria subulata var. subulata
*An excellent choice for providing
dense coverage in the middleground.*

Sagittaria subulata var. subulata

Dwarf Sagittaria
- **Substrate:** Open texture gravel
- **Lighting:** Moderate
- **pH value:** Not critical
- **Hardness:** Not critical
- **Temperature:** 13-26°C (55-79°F)

Height: 30cm (12in).
Distribution: Atlantic coast of North
America.
Characteristics: A grasslike plant
with leaves only 5mm (0.2in) wide.
These are bright green, with acute or
rounded tips. In shallow water, small
floating elliptical or egg-shaped
leaves are produced, followed by
small white flowers.
Aquarium use: Middleground. Set
out in groups of four to five plants. An
undemanding species that will soon
form dense stands in the right
conditions. It will succeed over a wide
temperature range and needs only
moderate lighting and an open
texture bottom gravel to thrive.
Propagation: By runners.
Other species: There are numerous
Sagittaria species, many of which
have several varieties. Some of these
are very small, forming a turf only
2.5cm (1in) high; others are giants
over 1m (39in) tall.

Salvinia auriculata

Butterfly Fern
- **Substrate:** Not applicable
- **Lighting:** Very bright
- **pH value:** Not critical
- **Hardness:** Not critical
- **Temperature:** 18°C (64°F)
  minimum

Height: A floating plant that lies flat
on the surface.
Distribution: Tropical America.
Characteristics: A perennial floating
fern, with horizontally growing, much-
branched shoots. The leaves, 3-4cm
(1.2-1.6in) long, are oval to egg-
shaped and are covered with fine
protective hairs. The third leaf in each
whorl of three is modified to form a
finely divided root structure. The
colour varies from bright green to
olive-green.
Aquarium use: As a shade-giving
plant and as a spawning site for
Anabantids and other fishes. In
common with most other floating
plants, *Salvinia* is very adaptable to
varying water conditions. It does
need abundant light, however. Under
natural daylight the plant grows very
large but it declines under inadequate
illumination in the aquarium. Protect
plants from condensation drips and
remove excess growth regularly to
prevent them casting too much
shade in the aquarium.
Propagation: This plant multiplies
freely from continuous branching and
the breaking away of lateral and
terminal shoots.

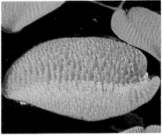

Above and right: **Salvinia auriculata**
A top view and close up of this rapidly spreading floating plant. Note the fine protective hairs on the leaf surface. Sensitive to condensation drips falling on to the top of the plant.

Below: **Samolus parviflorus**
Aptly named 'water cabbage', this subtropical plant creates striking rosettes of light green leaves.

Samolus parviflorus
Water Cabbage
- **Substrate:** Plain washed gravel
- **Lighting:** Bright
- **pH value:** Not critical
- **Hardness:** Not critical
- **Temperature:** 21°C (70°F) maximum

Height: Up to 10cm (4in).
Distribution: North America, West Indies and South America.
Characteristics: An amphibious water plant that grows in the form of a rosette and really does resemble a small cabbage. The light green, tongue-shaped leaves are 10cm (4in) long and 5cm (2in) wide. The inflorescence is a raceme with tiny white flowers. Submerged, however, only adventitious plantlets are formed.
Aquarium use: A foreground to middleground contrast plant. Grow it in an emersed state in pots of heavy soil containing a proportion of clay. When fully grown, transfer the plants to a well-lit position in the aquarium. It is really a subtropical species and so

the temperature should not exceed the recommended maximum. It tolerates hard water conditions well.

Propagation: When grown emersed, it will flower freely and produce thousands of seeds that germinate readily in damp soil. The seedlings develop quickly and may be potted up after a few weeks. After seeding, the flower stems produce several adventitious plantlets, which may be separated and potted up. As a third method of propagation, simply divide adult plants into several pieces.

Saururus cernuus
Lizard's Tail
- **Substrate:** Plain washed gravel
- **Lighting:** Not critical
- **pH value:** Not critical
- **Hardness:** Not critical
- **Temperature:** 24°C (75°F) maximum

Height: Up to 1m (39in) as a terrestrial plant, smaller when growing in the aquarium.
Distribution: Eastern North America.
Characteristics: A perennial swamp plant. The erect stems carry opposed heart-shaped leaves, up to 12cm

Above: **Saururus cernuus**
Use this North American plant as a temporary subject in the aquarium.

(4.7cm) long on short petioles. The younger leaves are hairy, but lose this as the plant matures. Leaf colour varies from light to dark green. The common name refers to the spiked inflorescence of tiny yellowish white flowers, borne on terrestrial plants only, not on submerged specimens.
Aquarium use: As a temporary specimen plant in smaller aquariums or massed among Cryptocorynes and similar plants in the middleground. Transfer cuttings about 20cm (8in) long to the aquarium, where they will root and grow quite well for a few months.
Propagation: By cuttings and runners, the latter freely produced.

Synnema triflorum
(Also Hygrophila difformis)
Water Wisteria
- **Substrate:** Plain washed gravel
- **Lighting:** Bright
- **pH value:** Not critical
- **Hardness:** Not critical
- **Temperature:** 20°C (68°F) minimum

Height: Up to 45cm (18in).
Distribution: Southeast Asia.
Characteristics: A very variable plant. The shoots may grow horizontally for a time before turning upwards. In emerse-grown plants the leaves are grey-green, small and simple. Submerged leaves, however, are very variable, with indentations and pinnate parts that give the plant an overall fernlike appearance. These leaves are light green, up to 10cm (4in) long and 8cm (3.2in) wide.

Aquarium use: A background and corner plant. Use three of four stems planted close together. This is a popular plant because of its versatility. It makes no special demands as to substrate or water chemistry, but does need a well-illuminated aquarium to thrive.
Propagation: By cuttings.

Below: **Synnema triflorum**
A very popular, easy-care plant with variable foliage and fresh colour.

Telanthera lilacina

Red Telanthera

- **Substrate:** Plain washed gravel
- **Lighting:** Bright
- **pH value:** Not critical
- **Hardness:** Not critical
- **Temperature:** 20°C (68°F) minimum

Height: Up to 30cm (12in).
Distribution: Tropical South America.
Characteristics: A marsh plant that also grows well submersed. The lanceolate leaves, up to 6cm (2.4in) long, are carried on short petioles and set in opposition on the stem. The upper surface of the leaf blade is in various shades of dark green, often with reddish tinges; the underside is pink to dark red.
Aquarium use: As a contrast plant in both middleground and background groupings, where its bright red coloration may be used to dramatic effect. Be sure to provide abundant light to sustain the plant's rich colour.
Propagation: By cuttings.

Below: **Telanthera lilacina**
Outstanding colour to dazzle the eye among more restrained shades.

Trichoronis rivularis
Mexican Oak-leaf Plant
- **Substrate:** Plain washed gravel
- **Lighting:** Bright to subdued
- **pH value:** Not critical
- **Hardness:** Not critical
- **Temperature:** 20°C (68°F) minimum

Height: Up to 30cm (12in).
Distribution: Mexico.
Characteristics: A herbaceous plant that produces trailing stems when grown emerse and upright stems when grown submerged. The thick stems bear opposite, light to dark green oval leaves with many indentations that give the laminae a toothed effect, hence the common name reference to oak leaves.
Aquarium use: As a middleground to background bunch plant. The attractively shaped leaves provide a refreshing contrast to other foliage types. This newly introduced species grows well in aquarium conditions.
Propagation: Take cuttings or detach plants produced on runners.

Below: **Trichoronis rivularis**
A new introduction with attractively toothed leaves. Extremely adaptable.

Above: **Vallisneria spiralis**
An elegant and easy plant that is familiar to aquarists the world over. An excellent background subject.

Vallisneria spiralis
Straight Vallisneria
- **Substrate:** Plain washed gravel
- **Lighting:** Bright
- **pH value:** Not critical
- **Hardness:** Not critical
- **Temperature:** 15-30°C (59-86°F)

Height: Up to 60cm (24in), although normally much smaller.
Distribution: Southern Europe and North Africa. Now introduced to many tropical and subtropical countries around the world.
Characteristics: The linear grasslike leaves – 4-8mm (0.16-0.32in) wide and pale to mid green in colour – are arranged in a rosette. The flowers are borne on a long, tightly spiralled stem, from which the plant derives its common name.
Aquarium use: A splendid and most popular aquatic species for background planting in tall aquariums. An undemanding plant that needs a brightly illuminated position but will also tolerate light shade. Indifferent to water quality in the aquarium.
Propagation: By runners, which are produced in abundance.

Above: **Vallisneria tortifolia**
The distinctively spiralled leaves add interest to this adaptable aquarium plant. Ideal for the middleground.

Varieties: *Vallisneria spiralis* var. Contortionist, a variety with more tightly spiralled leaves than *V. tortifolia* (see below) and which needs higher temperatures than the type to thrive in the aquarium.

Vallisneria tortifolia
Twisted Vallisneria
- **Substrate:** Plain washed gravel
- **Lighting:** Bright
- **pH value:** Not critical
- **Hardness:** Not critical
- **Temperature:** 15-30°C (59-86°F)

Height: Up to 20cm (8in).
Distribution: Originally Portugal, but now widely distributed in tropical and subtropical regions.
Characteristics: Considered by many experts to be a variety of *Vallisneria spiralis*, this plant has tightly spiralled leaves and is a most attractive and popular aquatic subject throughout the world.
Aquarium use: Middleground bunch plant.
Propagation: By runners.
Other species: *Vallisneria asiatica* is like a larger version of *V. tortifolia*, with

serrated margins to the leaves.
Vallisneria gigantea from Southeast
Asia, a giant plant reaching 1m (39in)
in height, with leaves up to 2cm (0.8in)
wide. The red variety is a most
attractive plant.

There is some confusion as to the
correct nomenclature of many of
these Vallisnerias. Some are claimed
as species by certain authorities;
others as hybrids.

Vesicularia dubyana

Java Moss
- **Substrate:** Rocks, bogwood, etc
- **Light:** Subdued
- **pH value:** Not critical
- **Hardness:** Not critical
- **Temperature:** 24°C (75°F)
  minimum

Height: A creeping species.
Distribution: Widely distributed in
tropical Southeast Asia.
Characteristics: A handsome moss
that forms tangled masses of
intensively branched stems clothed
with small leaves, light to dark green
in colour depending on the lighting
intensity. It thrives in dim light.

Above: **Vesicularia dubyana**
*A true moss that clings to rocks and
bogwood. Creates an intriguing 'soft
green shape' in the aquarium.*

Aquarium use: Grown attached to
rocks and bogwood, *Vesicularia* is
very useful for softening the harsh
effect of tank furnishings. In the wild,
this species is often found growing in
association with *Microsorium
pteropus*, Java Fern (see page 96),
and the combination also succeeds
well in aquariums.
Propagation: Simply pull clumps
from the parent mass and attach
them to their new location with a
rubber band or by placing a small
pebble on top. The filaments, or
hyphae, soon become attached by
means of rootlike structures known
as hapterons.
Other species: The genus contains
about 130 species, with several
aquatic members in Africa and
Southeast Asia. However, collectors
often send in mosses under the name
of 'Java Moss' that are wrongly
named and do not survive under
water. Check this with your dealer.

Index to plants

Page numbers in **bold** indicate major references, including accompanying photographs. Page numbers in *italics* indicate other illustrations. Less important text entries are shown in normal type.

R

S

T

U

V

W

Picture Credits

Artists
Copyright of the artwork illustrations on the pages following the artists' names is the property of Salamander Books Ltd.

Clifford and Wendy Meadway: 13, 38-39, 40-41, 42-43, 44-45, 51, 53, 58.

Photographs
The publishers wish to thank the following photographers who have supplied photographs for this book. The photographs have been credited by page number and position on the page: (B) Bottom, (T) Top, (C) Centre, (BL) Bottom left etc.

David Allison: 96(T), 98

Eric Crichton © Salamander: 16, 21, 24(T), 24-5(B), 29(B), 32-33, 33(T), 34, 35, 36, 37, 47, 50(T), 51(T), 52(T)

Barry James: Endpapers, 38(T), 39(T), 41, 45, 67(B), 71(T), 80, 87(B), 90-91(B), 109, 112, 113

Jan-Eric Larsson: Copyright page, 30-31, 59(B), 62, 64, 65(B), 72(T)

Chris Mattison: 40(BL)

Arend van den Nieuwenhuizen: 10-11, 56-57, 65(T), 68, 73(C), 76, 82, 94

Kurt Paffrath: 63, 67(T), 69, 70, 71(B), 72(B), 75(T,B), 77(TR), 78-9(B), 79(T), 83, 84(T,B), 85, 88(B), 92(T), 96-7(B), 99, 101, 102, 103(T), 104, 105, 106, 107(T), 108, 110

Mike Sandford: Half-title, Title page

David Sands: 14-15

William A. Tomey: 12, 22, 23, 28, 52(B), 60, 73(T), 77(TL), 81, 86, 87(T), 88(T), 89, 91(T), 92(B), 93, 95, 100, 103(B), 107(B), 111

Dr Jörg Vierke: 43, 74

Lothar Wischnath: 48

Rudolf Zukal: 49, 50(B), 59(T), 61(T,B), 66

Acknowledgements
The publishers wish to thank Philips Electronics/Lighting Division for their help in preparing this book.

Companion volumes of interest:

A Fishkeeper's Guide to THE TROPICAL AQUARIUM
A Fishkeeper's Guide to COMMUNITY FISHES
A Fishkeeper's Guide to COLDWATER FISHES
A Fishkeeper's Guide to MARINE FISHES
A Fishkeeper's Guide to MAINTAINING A HEALTHY AQUARIUM
A Fishkeeper's Guide to GARDEN PONDS
A Fishkeeper's Guide to CENTRAL AMERICAN CICHLIDS
A Petkeeper's Guide to REPTILES AND AMPHIBIANS

A plant farm in Singapore